Lewis Burd Walker, William Allen

Extracts from Chief Justice William Allen's Letter Book

Lewis Burd Walker, William Allen

Extracts from Chief Justice William Allen's Letter Book

ISBN/EAN: 9783337425258

Printed in Europe, USA, Canada, Australia, Japan

Cover: Foto ©Suzi / pixelio.de

More available books at **www.hansebooks.com**

The Burd Papers.

EXTRACTS

FROM

CHIEF JUSTICE WILLIAM ALLEN'S

LETTER BOOK.

SELECTED AND ARRANGED

BY

LEWIS BURD WALKER.

TOGETHER WITH AN APPENDIX
CONTAINING PAMPHLETS

IN

THE CONTROVERSY WITH
FRANKLIN.

1897.

COPYRIGHT 1897
BY
LEWIS BURD WALKER.

PREFACE.

Chief Justice William Allen was born August 5th, 1704. His mother, Mary, daughter of Thomas and Susanna Budd, was a sister of Rose Budd, whose daughter, Sarah Plumley, was married to Edward Shippen, of Lancaster. William Allen was married February 16, 1733—1734, to Margaret Hamilton, daughter of Andrew Hamilton, by whom he had four sons and two daughters, as follows:

John Allen, born about March, 1739; died February, 1778.

Andrew Allen, born June, 1840; died March 7, 1825.

James Allen, born about 1742; died September 19, 1778.

William Allen, born about 1751; died July 2, 1838.

Anne Allen, married May 31, 1766, to John Penn; died after August, 1813.

Margaret Allen, married August 19, 1771, to James de Lancey; died October 18, 1827.

In October, 1735, William Allen was chosen Mayor of Philadelphia, and on October 2, 1750, was appointed Chief Justice of Pennsylvania, which office he resigned in 1774, having received an annual salary of about £120, which he distributed in charity. It is to William Allen that the present location of the State House is due, as he purchased the ground with his own money, and held it until the province was able to reimburse him.

He was ever ready to assist men of talent who were struggling with adversity; and Benjamin West has expressed his lively sense of gratitude to William Allen in the strongest words, for the unexpected and unsolicited advance of money, which enabled West to complete his course of study in Italy. He also aided Franklin very materially, as will be seen by the letter to David Barclay & Sons, dated November 5, 1753, and by the "Answer to Mr. Franklin's Remarks," (attributed to Rev. William Smith), as published in the Appendix: and it is a matter of great regret that gratitude for favors received did not prevent Franklin from abusing his benefactor.

Though William Allen was strongly opposed to the tyrannical course pursued by the British Government towards America, and even contributed "cannon shot" for the use of the Board of the Council of Safety ; yet he was opposed to the Declaration of Independence, and therefore was considered a Tory.

He was a very extensive land-owner in Pennsylvania ; and upon one tract a town was laid out, which commemorates its founder in its present name of Allentown. He died Sept., 6th, 1780 ; and his letter book passed into the hands of Edward Shippen, afterwards Chief Justice. After the death of Edward Shippen it was handed over to Edward Burd, and from him to his daughter, Miss Sarah Burd.

After Miss Burd's death the next owners, Misses Mary and Louisa Hubley gave it to their nephew, Dr. Lewis L. Walker, subsequent to whose decease it came into the hands of his nephew, the present editor. This Book, bound in leather, contains copies of 187 letters of William Allen, covering the period of 1753-1770 ; from 87 of which extracts or copies have been made, which are herein published. In the appendix will be found a reprint of three scarce pamphlets, which are explanatory of some of the letters. The original spelling of the letters has been retained.

EXTRACTS

FROM

WILLIAM ALLEN'S LETTERS.

July 31, 1753. To B. Hume, P. Valette and P. Furnal.
The Sugars were consigned to Messrs. John & Thomas Simpson, whose unhappy Fate, no doubt, you must have heard; The former having shot himself & the latter so shocked at his Unckle's untimely End, that he took to his Bed & died in a few days.

Oct. 21, 1753. To D. Barclay & Sons, London.
I note what you write about the Lottery Tickets. As I do not like the Scheme of the Lottery should be glad this came in time to contradict my former Directions. I intend the Money should be laid in the first Government Lottery upon the usual footing. But as there is so large a Deduction to be taken out of this, it will no doubt be unprofitable to the Adventurers. However if this shall come too late, I shall be contented with what you do. I request you would Order my Periwig Maker to make me three Bob Wigs of the same Colour with the last, and forward them to me by any Opportunity that offers.

Nov. 5, 1753. To Evan Patterson, Atty. London.
* * * What I have from time to time charged you as a Commission, is what every merchant in America charges for the Receipt & Remittance of Money or only for Remittance :—Two and a half (per cent) being generally added for the Receipt, & often Five which in the whole would make Ten, But as I often thought that unreasonable, I never charged more than five under which (upon Inquiry) you'll find no money ever remitted by Bill or otherwise from America. * * * * I am willing to purchase their (the heirs of Bellair) interest in this Province which is One Hundred Acres of Liberty Land & Rights to 8000 acres of unlocated Land. I can with great truth inform you that their Rights are decaying in value every day, and are not worth now so much by forty per cent as they were twenty years ago: The Reason if attended to is very plain ; Because other people have taken up their Land. And the proprietors have since that time sold some Millions of Acres, at the Rate of fifteen pounds ten shillings this money a hundred in Small Tracts, even from twenty five Acres or upwards, so that all the good Land within the tract purchased of the Indians is taken up. There is an Expectation that within a few years another purchase may be made of the Indians, in which the Rights to land may be laid out to some advantage; tho' they must be very remote and not within one hundred & fifty miles of this City. Yet if care is taken and by persons well acquainted in the Country, some good Lands may be got. But if the Heirs of the Family do not sell before that time, or get some very judicious person immediately after it to locate their Lands, which will I can assure you be a very difficult Task, their Rights will be of no value ; they will be oblidged to lay out their land in some part of the Country,

now in the possession of the French, for they have lately built Forts within the bounds of this province. Upon the whole I mean that if they keep their Lands another twenty years in their Hands, the whole 8000 Acres will not be worth Fifty Guineas. As I am well acquainted with the back parts of the Country by Information from some who have been upon the Spot, I am willing to give them £800 for their Interest, & will remit them the money for the same, as soon as I am informed the Heirs are willing to sign the Deeds. I am no way anxious about the purchase, being assured I shall make no great matter of advantage by it. However that matter may be, this Information I give may be of some use to them, which may be depended on that if they let matters continue upon the Foot they have done, their Interest will vanish, of which I desire you would be so good as to acquaint them & me of their Result.

I would have made them offers for their Lands in the Jerseys; But that Province is in so distracted a Condition, and so little Hopes of it being otherwise as long as the present Governor lives, that nobody will venture to lay down any Sum for purchases there. All Lands in the Jerseys belonging to Gentlemen in England, or this, or the Neighboring provinces are taken possession of by a set of Freebooters, whom you cannot dislodge; But upon any attempt to remove them by Law rise up in Bodies, and in a riotous manner break open prisons and rescue persons arrested.

I have nearly thirty thousand acres in that province, which is mostly occupied by these Villians.

Nov. 5, 1753. To Thomas Simpson in London.

I have received your melancholy Letters. And give me leave to say the shocking News of my good Old Friend

your Father's Death gave me inexpressible Concern.
There was scarce any man in the World but my very
nearest Relations, for whom I had so great a regard.
The great Civilities I received from him, whilst I was
last in England; The many repeated Acts of Friendship,
all rivitted by a twenty four years Correspondence carried
on to our Mutual Satisfaction, had greatly indeared him
to me. He was one of the best the worthiest of men,
the compleatest Merchant I ever knew. I would have
as soon thought, the Monument would have fallen, as he
have failed in his Circumstances. What can have produced this Revolution in his affairs, or how so frugal, so
knowing & exact a man can have been reduced, I can by
no means imagine. I had a hint given me about five
years ago, from a friend of mine in London, that his
affairs were in disorder, but I could by no means credit
it, and indeed that very account was contradicted by the
same person about six month after.

I am in a great measure got out of trade, which I by
experience find cannot be readily carried on to Profit, so
that my Connexions with your worthy Father have been
nothing near so considerable as formerly, but still the
House is indebted to Allen & Turner & to me about
£1700 Sterling, which Sum we must endeavor to secure,
by the Sale of his Lands, by due Course of Law; of which
there remains in this Province unsold, two Tracts one of
1800 acres, Another of 550 acres. * * * * * * *
* * There remains in the Jerseys unsold upwards of
Six thousand acres. But there are so many Disputes
between the Bounds of the Eastern & Western Division,
and such a Confusion among the Inhabitants about their
Titles, of which I formerly apprized your Father, that I
cannot say much of the Value. I am in hopes that a good

part of our Debt, will be secured by the Lands in this
Province and that in the Jerseys may remain clear to you.

I have already by the sale of the Lands remitted your
good Father more considerably than all his Lands both
here and in the Jerseys cost him. And as this was a
Scheme I advised him to and by my assistance they were
surveyed and located in beneficial Places, I hope you will
think it but right, that I should indeavour to secure myself what is owing to me out of them. He pressed me
to sell the Lands, but as he referred everything to my
Judgment I advised that they should remain, because I
thought they would rise in value, which has been
accordingly the Case, and what cost him but £350 being
five thousand acres. And one of the purchases will with
what I have already accounted with him for, amount to
near £2000.

Nov. 5, 1753.   To Isaac & Peter Carey, Merchants in
Guernsey.

I applyed to young Mr. Baynton, & his Father's Ex.
Mr. Maddox, and laid your accounts before them. They
on their part produced theirs, and made their Objections
to sundry parts of yours. Upon the whole I proposed
to them to leave the matter to Reference, which was
accordingly done by mutual Consent to a very honest
judicious man Mr. William Coleman a merchant of this
place. * * * I am concerned in a still House here
that we imagine makes much better Rum * * *
than the New England Rum.

        Philada. 5th Nov 1753.
Gentlemen

I wrote you by way of Ireland, and sent Copy of the
Same by way of Bristol, acknowledging your Sundry

favours and contradicting my former Orders about
investing the money of the South Sea Annuities in Lottery Tickets, upon account of the disadvantageous lay
the Adventurers must have—which I now confirm, I
had omitted to acquaint you that I shipped 1500 Bushells of Wheat on board the Ship Philadelphia Robert
Ferguson Master addressed to Messrs Butler & Mathews
in Cadiz and gave them Directions to ship you the Nt Proceeds. I now beg leave to request your favour in Behalf
of Mr. Benjamin Franklin: Who by Solicitations from me
to sundry of my friends has obtained the Office of being
joint Post Master with one Hunter in Virginia, of all
North America. As perhaps some Securities may be
expected for the due performance of his Office and
remitting any Overplus Money that may accrue after the
Officers Salaries are paid (Though hitherto that has
not been the Case, the Profits of the Post Office having
never amounted to so much as has been sufficient to pay
the Salaries and Charges.) But I am persuaded, that by
Mr. Franklin's good Management, matters will be put
upon a better footing, and that there will be yearly some
Ballance to be remitted to the general Post Office. I
therefore entreat you would be so kind as to call upon
Mr. Shelvock, the Secretary of the Post Office (who has
been instrumental in obtaining the Office) and inquire
whether any Security is necessary; and if it is that you
would either by yourself or Friends become his Security.
And upon your acquainting me that such Security is
given, and sending over a proper Bond to be signed by
Mr. Turner and me, we will counter Secure you.

I beg pardon for giving you this Trouble; but as it is
giving the finishing Stroke to an affair I have had much
at heart, I beg you would be so good as to excuse it:
And your kindness herein I shall always greatly

acknowledge. Inclosed you have a Letter for Messrs Isaac & Peter Carey of Guernsey, which please to forward to them, in whose favour I have drawn a Bill on you for £89 11s 6. and also another of this Date in favour of Alexr Stuart both which please to pay. As you will no doubt hear fully from Allen & Turner of the Remittances we are making you by Bills on Paris, and that the proceeds of Nicaragua Wood & Iron sent to Bristol are ordered into your Hands, it will be needless for me to say anything further but to assure you I always am

  Gentlemen
   Your Most Obt Humble Servt
    WILLIAM ALLEN.

P. S. Since writing the above I find Mr. Franklin has got his Commission & informs me that Mr. Hunter has found Security for them both.

To Messrs David Barclay & Sons.

Nov. 16, 1753. To Don Bernardo Ruiz de Norriega at Carthagena.

We could not meet with any Coach that we thought suitable. There was indeed an old one belonging to a former Governor, that we could have got fitted up for about one hundred pistoles that would have appeared like a new one, but was fearful it might not have suited. If such a One would be agreeable, upon your advising us we will get it ready again any other Opportunity, of which please to give us the earliest Notice as it will take a good deal of time to repair it. We have sent you Two Barrells of Apples 3 Dozen of choice Pontac Wine, 1 Dozen of Frontiniack, one large Parmesan Cheese, one cask of Gammons & two Bottles of East India Catchup, which we beg you would be so good as to accept of.

---

26 November, 1753. To D. Barclay & Son.

I request you would be pleased to buy for the Use of my Sons, of Mr. Strahan the Books of which you have herewith a List—And as I live in the Country in the Summer Season, and good part of my Amusement is a Kitchen Garden, pray be so kind as to send me the Seeds, a List of which you have here subjoined.

1 Gallon of each of the three best sorts of early Hotspur peas.

1 Peck of best early Readings

2 Oz. of early Battersea Cabbage

1 Oz. of the Russia, and one ounce of every sort of Cabbage that is esteemed to be very good & one ounce of each of the Savoy kind.

2 Ounces of Colly Flower.

Greek Books 3 Copies or Sets of Minores Poetae
    3 Do of Euchiridon's Epictetus
    1 Do of Stanhope's Epictetus
    1 Do of Arian's Epictetus
    1 Do of Avery's Epictetus
    3 Do of Xenephon's Cyropaedia
    3 Do of Homer by Clerk
    3 Do of Sophocles
    3 Do of King's Euripides
    3 Do of Pindar ye Oxford Edn Folio.
    3 Do of Longinus by Pearse.
    1 Do of Smith's Translation of Longinus
    3 Do of Antoninus by Gataker

3 Do of Potter's Antiquities
3 Do of Demosthenes Orations
3 Do of Thucidides
6 Do of Lucian by Murphy in 2 Vols.
2 Do of Taylor's Demosthenes.
3 Do of Winchester School Phrases
3 Do of Robertson's Phrase Book
3 Do of Walker on the Particles
3 Do of Willy's Notes.
3 Copies of Juvenal in usum Delphini.
3 Copies of Francis's Horace
3 Do of Virtots Revolutions of the Roman Empire.
3 Do of Plutarch's Lives.
3 Do of Rollin's Method of Studying the Belles Letters
3 Do of do Antient History in Octavo
& of his do on Arts & Sciences.
3 of Dryden's Juvenal
3 of Mr. Frolard in 6 vol 4to on the Roman's Arts of War.
Schanchii Chronologie
One Copy of the Compleat Collection of Voyages & Travells by John Haris 2 Vols Fol
The New Universal Dictionary of Arts & Sciences just published. Folio.

April 5, 1754. To Don B. Ruiz Norriege, Carthagena.
We are fitting up the Coach & will have it in readiness to send by next Opportunity. * * * At the desire of a particular Friend of ours, we beg leave to request you would be so good as to write to some friend of yours

at St. Iago de Cuba to procure the copy of the Condemnation of a Sloop taken in the late War. As we are instructed the Affair stands circumstanced in this manner.—About the 27th of March 1746, a Sloop named the Watts, Joseph Arthur, junior, Master, belonging to Samuel McCall Senr of this Place was taken on her Voyage from hence to Jamaica, in the Windward Passage by the famous Spanish Row Galley, Capt Possant, Commander, and by him sent to St Iago de Cuba, where very soon after, she was condemned as lawful prize, and together with her Cargo was sold in that port. The Owner had some Insurance made on said Sloop in Holland. But the Assurers have refused hitherto to pay any part of the Loss, because no Copy of the Condemnation has been procured from under the Seals of the proper Office or Officer at St. Iago de Cuba. * * You are therefore prayed * * * to * * send two Copies of said Condemnation of Sloop Watts.

April 20, 1754. To Edmund Butler at the Temple London.

The three houses in Chestnut Street sold for the following Sums viz one of them for £117 16s 6d. another for £250 and the third for £650. and the five hundred Acres of land in this County for £750. (all Pennsylvania Currency); All which, I think well sold.

April 20, 1754. To Evan Pattorson.

I shall be expecting Answers from the Heirs of Bellairs to my Proposals by Shirley. At the same time, please to acquaint them that a new Indian Purchase is like to be made some time this Summer, and that if I do not purchase the Land early enough to be able to locate the Rights in the New Purchase, I would not give a Quarter of the Sum I offer; For all the good Land will be taken up and Rights to Land will be of a trifling Value. I offered all the money I am inclined to give, which is £800 for the Liberty Land and 8000 as of Rights to Land. And I am persuaded they never will make more of it.

April 20, 1754. To D. Barclay & Sons.

I perceive that the Lottery Tickets are all Blanks, to which I have little to say, but that my Luck in the English Lottery is not so good as that of some others, And I am quite satisfied with what you have done being persuaded you acted for the best.

I have received the Books in good Order, as likewise your kind presents to my Children of the Sleeve Buttons, for which pray give me leave to return you my hearty thanks. I find by imitating the example of your worthy Father & partner I must employ another Factor for these Triffles, for I can never learn the Cost of them, which, was I not assured of your Friendship & good Will, would be very disagreeable to me. * * * I was truly concerned to hear of the Indisposition of my much esteemed Friend Mr. David Barclay, Senior; But hope from some of your late Letters this will find him restored to health, which will give high pleasure to many good people here.

June 27, 1754. To Don Bernardo Ruiz.

We are glad to find that Mr. (John) Gibson has behaved to your Satisfaction. As he was bred in our Counting House, we can by a sufficient Experience pronounce him a man of Honesty & Candour. * * * We beg you would endeavour to procure for us some Balsam Copabia & some of the Earth to cure Ringworms. We have bought the Coach according to your Directions and have got it fitted up in the best manner we could ; But as we were at a Loss in what way you would have it painted, We have only done it with One Colour, Mr. Gibson telling us that you could get it done, with you, to your Mind. We have given for it, only 80 Pistoles, being 20 less than we expected. We wish it safe to your Hands & that it may be to your liking.

October 2, 1754. Col. John Chiswell, of Virginia.

In answer to your desire of borrowing the sum of £2000 Sterling at Six per Cent ; Give me leave to say that at present we have among us ten Borrowers to One Lender : and very few of the latter chuse to lend any money without the Province ; As they cannot readily at a Distance command a punctual payment of their Interest. In the Neighboring Provinces their Interest is Seven p Cent. Yet our People had rather have Six within the Province for the Reason above. I am confident that Such a Sum as you mention cannot be obtained on Interest for any Security without the Province. Indeed Money is not near so plenty as it was during the War, and some few years after, at which time there was money Lenders, who now chuse to employ their Stocks in Trade.

December 12, 1754. To Don Bernardo at Carthagena.

We have been endeavouring to buy you a couple of large white Horses, but cannot meet with any that are suitable, if those of another Colour will do we will procure the best we can. We hope by this time you have been able to procure for us the Terra Macamachica, &

must beg you would send us ½ Dozen pound of a Root called Siena Raba, it being useful in Fluxes & a long settled laxed State of Body. We are told it is the produce of your Country, or somewhere along the Coast. The Dutch frequently bringing it to Curacoa from the Coast, we shall be much obliged to you, if you will take some pains to get it for us, being greatly Sollicited by our Physicians here to write for it

December 12 1754. To Don Juan Arrecharreta at Carthagena.

We have Opportunities almost every week either to London or Lisbon and frequently to Cadiz any Letters you are pleased to send by Vessels returning here from your place shall be forwarded with the greatest Care.

December 23, 1754. To Evan Patterson.

As I have not heard any more of Bellair's Lands I decline making the purchase. The Land lately bot of the Indians is in a great part possessed by the French, they having lately invaded the Province & built three Forts in the back parts, and what is not already in their possession is, at present in so precarious a Situation, that I do not care to venture to buy any more Land here, having too much already at Stake. The French finding that our Quakers will not defend the Country seem to be about to take possession of this Province, which they will inevitably do, if we are not succoured from England.

March 18 1755. To Don Bernardo Ruiz.

We have by this Vessell sent you a Doz. of Saltpetre Hams, a Flitch of Bacon, 100 lb of Dryed Beef, a Dozen of Tongues, an English Cheese, a Dozen of Claret & a

Dozen of White Wine, which we beg you would be so
kind as to accept: we shall be waiting your Orders
about the Horses you would have shipped.

May 18 1755. To David Barclay & Sons.

Capt Thinn is a Scotch Gentleman who went with the
Command of a Company to Carthagena from this place,
was an acquaintance of Mr. Hamiltons, is married to a
Wealthy Poulterer's Widow at the other End of the
Town, & must be known to the Scotch Officers & I am
told frequents the British Coffee House, was upon Half
Pay, but has sold out.

I beg you would bespeak three Bob-wigs of my barber,
& that you would send me by the first Vessell, a Groce
of the freshest Pyrmont Water. As it is intended for
Mr. Hamilton & me, I beg you would be very careful
that it be of the very last Importation. * * * I have
a very high Opinion of the Mine, which mends every
Day.

May 23, 1755. To John Barclay, Dublin.

Having seen in the Universal Magazine of July last
an account of a Mine in Ireland by W. Henry D. D. ex
tracted from the Philosophical Transactions at Crone
Bawn, near the Town of Arklow in the County of Wick-
low, which affords a Water out of the Level of said mine
that dissolves Iron, and makes the Copper with which
this Water is impregnated, precipitate, so as to produce
great Quantities thereof. We take the freedom to request you would be pleased to make a minute Inquiry
nto this matter, what profit is made yearly of this
Water; how the precipitated Copper is melted, in what
kind of a Furnace, whether the Bellows goes by Water,
or whether it is what they call an Air Furnace: what

Fuel is used in the melting, and what Flux, or if any is used—And, if you can, procure a Draught of the Pits where the Iron is placed, and how the Water is let out, in order to get out the Copper Dust (the Magazine informing us how it is carried into the Pits) and whether any Workmen can be got, particularly those who understand the building the Furnaces and melting the Copper, that understand the whole Process, and at what Rate they would come over here to be hired for four years certain, and whether any sober able-bodied Miners can be procured to come over here & upon what terms. The Reason of our giving you this Trouble, is that we are concerned One Third in a Copper Mine in this Province, that affords a Spring whose Qualities are the same with that above mentioned, but much Stronger, as it will dissolve Iron in a Quarter part of the Time, and yield the same yellowish Copper Mud or Dust, which, melted in a Crucible, produces about half pure Copper.

This Spring comes through an immense Body of Vitriol Ore—a small quantity of it (it is apprehended) will, if taken inwardly kill a Man—when lowered with common Water, it is used frequently for purging and vomiting the Country people, is useful for curing Ulcers & cutaneous Disorders, and particularly for sore Eyes. From the Spring flows about 7 or 800 Hhds. in twenty four hours, consequently it is sufficient to fill as many pits as we please.

We have not worked the Mine for some years, this Vitriolic Spring having been so prominent, that we could not clear it of water. We never got any large Vein of Copper; But to Sulphur & Vitriol Ore there was no End.

As you may perhaps be acquainted with some of the Proprs of the mine at Crone Bawn, or by a proper

Inquiry you may be able we are in hopes, to return to us, by Letter a Satisfactory Accot of this matter.

May 23 1755.   To D. Barclay & Sons.

We have some Thoughts of building a Furnace for melting our poor Copper Ore. And as we are not sure of Bricks made of a proper Clay fit to bear the hot Fire of Furnace we beg you would endeavour to procure 3000 Bricks fit for that Use. We are told they are got near Windsor; however that you will be best assured of upon Inquiry. I hope they may be got for an easy Freight as they will serve as ballast. Please to ship them by any Opportunity that offers this Fall.

Governor Fisher has wrote on my Behalf to Mr. Sydenham at the end of Catherine Street in the Strand for 12 Dishes & Six Dozen of Plates of a particular kind of pewter.

June 15, 1755.   To Don Bernardo Ruiz.

Dr. Ross is lately gone to New York, so that we could not get his Opinion of the Quality of the (Jesuits') Bark. Our other Doctors say it is not of the first Sort. * * * As there is a probability of a French War, we must beg for the future that you would not send any more Bar Gold, for as we are obliged to ship it to London, the Insurance will run high.

July 7, 1755.   To D. Barclay & Son.

As we are just returned from the Mine, and have had a Sight of yours to Captain Stevens of the 19th of March, in which you send the Report of the Essay-Master on the 90 Barrells, I take the liberty to desire you would get tried, all the Ore that has gone since that was shipped, as it comes all out of the same Vein, as did, that Barrell, in which you say Gold is found.

And though the Ore is grown harder, as it goes into the Hill, and richer in Copper yet it retains the same dark Colour. And what further confirms us, is, that as we have the Stamping Mill now agoing, we have been able to discern small Specks of Gold in the Ore after it is stamped, and in a very little Vein, that runs close by the large Vein, we have discovered some Specks of Gold. Our Stamp Ore according to our Trials here yields near Two Thirds Copper. We are a little hindered by the dry Weather, there not being Water sufficient for our Mill, or should have shortly a large Quantity on hand, we stamped about Three tuns the Ten days we worked. We are at a loss whether to proceed to stamp any more, as the five Barrells you mention to yield 500 lb to the Tun are from our Stamp Ore, and we have above Ground, we think, at least 2000 Tuns, not much, if anything inferior in Quality. We are apt to think it would be more for our Interest to ship it without Stamping, as it is so valuable. I wish you would be so kind to inquire, whether a person, who is used to melting of Ore in a large Furnace could not be procured to come over here & upon what Terms, for as we have a prodigious quantity of that Sort of inferior Ore, we would keep a Furnace constantly going.

And as our Ore is chiefly of a soft Nature, full of Verdigrease, we fear it will lose considerably in the Washing, & that the Verdigrease will run off with the Water. We have neglected to work of late upon this Sort, of which there is a vast Body, as we wrote you formerly, and are now wholly imployed in following the Vein of blackest Ore, & are carrying up a Level—As that

Vein increases in Quantity and Quality, we are in hopes, if it continues to improve as it has done for these last two Months, or even continues as it is now, to get out, at least, a hundred Barrells of Firsts & Seconds a Month, besides Stamp Ore. The Vein of all three Sorts, being eight feet wide, & we already know it to be near 20 Feet up and down, being now at work upon it in 5 Sloops & we leave it over Head and under Feet.

Upon the whole we cannot but think it to be the greatest discovery of this Sort that has been found out in these parts of the World. * * * Please likewise to send an Account of the Produce of the small bags, that had the Ore in which was found Gold. This they have been long desirous to hear the Upshot of. * * * Please to send by any Vessell this Fall
a peck of early Hotspur Peas.
Do of early Readings.
Do of Windsor Beans.

July 21, 1755. To D. Barclay & Sons.

The late Defeat of the King's Forces has put every thing in the greatest confusion in this Province, to the great Scandal of the English Name. General Braddock with an advanced part of his Army was attacked by one Third of his Number of Indians & French & put to the Rout; one half of his party either killed or wounded; his Military Chest with £25,000 Sterling, all his Artillery, Baggage, Papers &c lost to the Enemy. And what is scarce to be credited, the Remainder of his Army was in such a pannick, that they retreated after having destroyed all the Ammunition & Provisions, and brought off only with them two Six Pounders of all the fine Train, Sent out of England. This last part of their Conduct is still more unaccountable than all the rest. If the Train or Ammunition had been preserved, the Americans were so enraged, that they would of themselves, have raised a Sufficient Number of men to dislodge the French men.

Could our Assembly be prevailed on to raise the Money, not less than 3000 men would have gone out of this Province; who as they fight for their Country, and are more used to the Woods & have a better notion of the Indian method of Fighting, would behave in another manner than the English Troops have done. The General sent over (who is now dead of his wounds) was quite an improper man, of a mean Capacity, obstinate and self-sufficient, above taking advice, & laughed to scorn all such as represented to him that in our Wood Country, war was to be carried on in a different manner from that in Europe. Nothing, he thought could stand his Veterans. The private Soldiers behaved shamefully. The Officers acted like brave Men & were mostly killed or wounded.

As there is some appearance of our being roused from our Lethargy, we are about putting the Province in some small position of Defence. But as we are much in want of Arms, we are desired to send for a Thousand Musquets, which we are told may be bought at the Tower from 11s. to 13s. a piece with Bayonets & Cartouch Boxes, being such as the Army have formerly used. We are informed that the East India Company purchase such for their Settlements. We beg therefore that you would purchase the above Quantity, on the best Terms you can & Ship them by the very first Opportunity this Fall if possible, taking care they be well inspected that they are good & fit for Service, together with a Tun of Musquet Balls and get the whole insured.

August 9, 1755. To D. Barclay & Sons.

Please to send our William Allen The Chronology & History of the World from the Creation of the World to 1753 by the Revd John Blair L. L. D. in Folio.

Philada. October 25 1755. To Ferdinand Paris.

Sir: The present melancholy Situation of this Country has so alarmed our Inhabitants that they cannot longer remain silent, but think it their Duty to lay their Condition before his Majesty; they have therefore prepared the inclosed Petition, which I am directed to transmit to you. The terrible accounts we have received from Cumberland County of the murders committed there, & in the back parts of Virginia & Maryland have given Rise to the Petition at this Time; and as it was got ready but a few days before this Vessell sailed, we have not had time to get it signed by many persons, but some of the people of the best Consideration in this City. As the Season begins to be far advanced, we tho't it best to send one Copy with the Names already to it. Copies are gone up to several of the Counties; and we shall be able to send you by the next Opportunity another Copy with a great number of Hands. In the mean time I beg you would retain such Council as you shall think most proper. We presume the Attorney General, Mr. Hume Campbell, Mr. York, Mr. Forester (which last was, we hear Council for our Govr before the Board of Trade) may be suitable: However this we shall leave to you, desiring that two or three, at the most should be retained, among which we would have the Attorney General for one.

We all hope and assuredly depend that our Proprietors will give us all the Assistance in their power, as their Interest is so nearly connected with that of the Inhabitants. If the malevolent party that is opposed to their Interest & their Government do not receive a Check from England, both their power and Estate will be rendered very precarious; as there is a Conspiracy among the Leaders of the Opposition to destroy both as much as in them lies;—of all which, & who they are, no doubt you are sufficiently apprized from other Hands, I mean from the Letters sent to the Proprietors from Such as are immediately concerned in their Affairs. The petitioners are some of the most Zealous Friends to the proprietary Family; men in whose Breast all Traces of Gratitude are not effaced, but have a high Sense of the Obligations we are under to that Honbl Family for the ample Charter of priviledges received from our first worthy Proprietor, & count themselves happy to live under his Successor's just administration could it be preserved to us.

If we shall not be happy enough to have their Aid and Assistance, we know all our weak efforts will be in vain, and we shall have the mortification to be laughed to Scorn by their adversaries; who now have the Confidence to tell us that the Proprietors are well pleased with the Conduct of our Assembly, and are desirous we should continue in the same defenceless Condition. We cannot but with Horror see the Blood of our Fellow Subjects spilt by cruel Savages; and we are not a little alarmed to think we are in the greatest danger of losing our Fortunes & Liberties. I expect before the End of next Summer, if nothing is done (if an entire Conquest is not made of the Province) that all the people over Susquehannah who are upwards of 4000 Families, chiefly Scotch-Irish, will be driven from their Habitations, & when they come down among the Germans & Quakers there will be next to a Civil War among them.

Upon the whole I fear, even as matters now stand it will be impossible to preserve the peace of the Province for any time.

I am placed by the Government in a Station that makes this matter pretty immediately my care.—my place I would fain resign, but that I think it unworthy of a man to desert his Country in such difficulties. I fear the Laws, when things are gone to confusion, will be little regarded; no pains shall be wanting on my part, as far as I am concerned, to see them put in execution, in the most effectual manner possible.

If you think our Circumstances are such, that they need not the Weight of more Hands to our petition, in such case it will be best, to save time, to present it immediately.

But in case you should be of opinion that a great number of Signers, would be more regarded by his Majesty & his Ministers, you may be assured that we shall procure several Hundred, I believe I may venture to say a Thousand more Signers to the Copies that will be sent you by the Opportunities that may offer. As to Instructions to a Gentleman so well acquainted with the affairs of this province, we hardly think them necessary: however shall by other Conveyances write what we judge to be needful. The Allegations in our Petition are strictly true. The Remady we would request Is, that we may be included in the Bill for uniting the Colonies, & our Case properly provided for in the same, should that measure take Effect. If no such Bill passes this Session coming on, we would fain hope his Majesty & his Ministers will not suffer this Colony, Situate in the Center of his Majesty's American Dominions, to remain any longer defenceless, but will recommend it to the Parliament to restrain our Quakers & Germans from sitting in the House of Assembly & the latter from even voting, till they know our language and are better acquainted with our Constitution. These poor people are so poysoned by the false Stories of the Quakers that they will be absolutely under their Direction; Nothing less than this will be a sufficient Remedy; for otherwise we shall never be put into a proper posture of Defence; nor the Force of the Province exerted for the Common Cause. Some few of us have been put already to very great Expenses by a former petition & Since that in erecting a Fortification, purchasing of Arms &c. Therefore intreat you would be as frugal as possible in this Sollicitation, & disburse no money but what is absolutely necessary.

We flatter ourselves, as we conceive our Cause & that of the proprietaries is the same, that they would be so good as to help to alleviate the Charge, by contributing a part.

I have wrote to Mr Barclay & Sons to pay such Sums as you shall call upon them for towards this Service, which I trust you will make as little expensive as possible.

Our Case is so grievous, & at the same time so notorious that we would fain hope much need not be said or done to convince the Ministry of the Danger we are in, and the Disgrace that will accrue to Britain should we fall a pray to the Enemy which will be undoubtedly the Case if we are attacked by any Number of Men.

I have in a Hurry wrote you my crude Thoughts on

this Affair, & beg leave only to assure you, that I am,
Dear Sir,
    your affectionate Friend & most Humble Servt.

                                       W A

To
Ferdinando Paris Esq
at his House in Surry Street in the Strand
        London.

Oct 25 1755. To D. Barclay & Sons.

The frequent accounts of the cruel Murders committed in the back parts of Virginia & Maryland by the Indians, formerly belonging to this Province; who, as they found they were not likely to be supported by us against the French, have at length joined them. & have for some time greatly alarmed us, not knowing how soon it might be the case of our own Inhabitants. To our great concern we have accounts from Cumberland County in this Province this last Week that the Indians have mur dered & carried into Captivity near thirty People; which has caused a great Terror & Confusion among the People; they having very few Arms & no fortified places to Shelter themselves in. The Inhabitants therefore in this City & in most of the Counties in the Province have thought it their Duty to lay their distressed Condition before their Sovereign & prayed his gracious Interposition that they might be put into a position of Defence. A petition to that purpose is by this Opportunity Sent to Mr Paris to sollicit the same. I desire therefore you be pleased to pay him such Sums on my Acco't for that Service that he shall be under a necessity to call upon you for, and charge the same to me.

November 6 1755. To Don Bernardo Ruiz.

As Letters of Reprisals are granted, and near a Hundred Sail of French merchantmen carried into the English Ports, and War is long before this time declared between the two Nations; we do not doubt but you will think it right to allow us the War price. As some of the Vessells we send you may probably be intercepted by the French, it will be necessary to send us more passes that there may be no Failure or Interruption of our Commerce.

November 14 1755. To John Barclay, Dublin.

We are exceedingly obliged to you for the pains you have taken in the Enquiry about the Copper Water, which gives us no small Satisfaction. We have taken the Freedom to send you a Couple of Bottles of our Water, which we desire you would be pleased to show to some of those Gentlemen, who are acquainted with the Properties of that in the Mines with you. We should have sent you a larger quantity, but have not time to send into the Country for more. We are convinced the Water has very near the same Qualities with the Irish Water, but fear that the Vitriol is too predominant, & will consume the Iron too fast.

We are a Quarter concerned in a very valuable Copper Mine about 50 miles from this Town, in the province of New Jersey; and have now at work between 50 & 60 men; but as we are greatly in want of able & Skillful Miners, we should be glad you would engage for us 6 or 8 good Workmen such as are compleat Masters of their Business & understand boring and blasting. Our Ground being pretty hard & rocky we would chuse such as have been acquainted with sinking down Shafts & carrying on Levels, such as they call in Cornwall, Sump Men, who are used to sink Shafts when troubled with Water. As the Miners generally chuse to work in Mines where the Ore is plenty, & turns to profit—you may assure them ours is of such a Sort, we having got out upwards of a Thousand Barrells within these 12 mos. besides an immense Quantity of Stamp Ore. * * We shall be content to pay them £20 Sterling p Annum and find them in Lodgings & Victuals; Or give them 12s. Sterling a Month in Lieu of their Board, to be at their Option, provided they indent on these Conditions for 4 years, in which Case we will pay their passages over here.

November 25 1755.   To Ferdinando Paris.

The late Commotions in the Country & the Terror & Confusion the People are in, have been the Occasion why the Petitions from the back Country have not yet been sent to Town: However I do by this Opportunity transmit to you such as are come to Hand. I beg therefore if you have not presented the Petition sent by Capt. Robinson, you will immediately lay what is now sent before his Majesty. I presume as they are only copies there will be no necessity of presenting more than one, and keeping the rest only to be shown as vouchers of the Number who conceive themselves aggrieved. Petitions have been presented from all Quarters to our Assembly for the Defence of the Country, who have gone into a Solemn Farce, and made what they call a Melitia Law, impracticable & ridiculous & calculated rather to prevent than incourage persons to exert themselves in defence of their Country.

In case you should not think fit to solicit our petition of which I think there is no danger, tho' our people here

& indeed many of them are fearful that your Connection with the Proprietary Family may induce you to decline it. In such Case, they & I trust to your Honor, that you would employ some proper persons in our Behalf to transact our Affairs. For my part, I cannot suffer myself to be persuaded but that the Proprietors in compassion to the poor distressed people, & in regard to their own true Interest will co-operate with us on this Occasion. I need not particularly describe the Miseries of the Province, great part of which is already laid Waste, and if his Majesty does not graciously interpose will, in a little time, be quite ruined. I beg you would be so good with your wonted care & assuidity to do everything in your power to obtain a favorable Answer to our Petition. You will hereby confer a great Obligation on our Inhabitants.

November 27 1755. To Wm. Beckford Esq. Soho Square, London.

As I have the Honour to be intimately acquainted with a friend of yours Mr Wm Gordon of the Island of Jamaica, & am further imboldened by the great & Worthy Character you bear, I tho' a Stranger, have taken the Freedom to solicit your Favour in Behalf of this distressed Province.

We have of late been harrassed by the Incursions of bloody Savages, who have, for Some time past, ravaged the back parts of this Province, & laid it waste with Fire & Sword; by which means Thousands of Familys have been driven from their Habitations. These Miserys are chiefly owing to the defenceless State of the Province; —our Assemblys being filled with Quakers, who, by the influence they have over the German Foreigners, get themselves elected as our Representatives. From their avowed principles they surely are unfit for the Seats they fill, at least in time of War, being, as they say, principled against bearing Arms.

We have by Petition, laid our distressed Condition before his Majesty & prayed his gracious Interposition; and are in hopes, by aid of Parliament, to have our Grievances redressed. I do therefore intreat you, in behalf of this Province, that you would afford us your Countenance & Assistance. The Colonies in the several parts of America are so connected by Commerce & a mutual Dependance on one another for Support that one part cannot be destroyed without affecting the Other. As your large Possessions in Jamaica must, of course, make these parts of the World the Object of your Thoughts & Care; and as it cannot be unknown to you that we are the greatest Granary in America, should we be torn from the British Empire (which is too probable in case of a War with France, as more than One Third of it is already in possession of the Enemy) not only Britain but the West India Islands must be deeply affected.

Our Assembly, within these few days, being alarmed by the daily Incroachments of the Enemy, and frightened by the threats of the People, who vowed Vengeance against the Authors of their Miseries, have been induced to pass a Melitia Law, which is so absurd in itself, and so destructive of the Prerogatives of the Crown, that it is feared it will not answer, by any means, our Necessitys, as no person is obliged to regard it, and such as are willing to defend their Country are exposed to be treated in a different manner than any other Melitia in his Majesty's

Dominions, no Distinction being made between such as enlist for pay & are to be sent on any expeditions, and those who meet occasionally as they do in the rest of the Colonies.

One other Observation, I beg leave to make, is, that one half the inhabitants of this Province are Foreigners, and as they, by the Bill, have the Choice of their own Officers they cannot be supposed to be under a proper Dependance on the Crown of England, but may join the Enemy, or drive out the English Inhabitants. They have, in their own Country, generally been Soldiers, whereas the other Inhabitants, having lived under a Quaker Government are quite unexperienced in all military Matters. I have taken the freedom to inclose you three of our public papers, in which you will find this blessed Quaker Melitia Act, & some other Things that may help to give you a proper notion of our Affairs.

As I am sure you love your Country, and have a pleasure in having an Opportunity of rendering it Service, I shall make no further Apology for this Freedom, but only request you would be assured that I should be proud to receive your Commands, & that I am, Sir,

  Your Most Obedt Humble Servant
    W. Allen.

December 17 1755. To D. Barclay & Sons.

We are in the most deplorable Situation imaginable in this province, every day bringing fresh Accounts of the Murders committed by the Indians; and the pannick is so great that it affects the people within twenty miles of the Town. Some have been killed by them within 55 miles this Week. What a Deal have those Wretches to answer for, who, instead of putting the Province into a position of Defence have wasted the time in Senseless insignificant Disputes. They are in the End like to get their Reward, for they are heartily dispised and hated by the people & particularly by the Germans who were formerly much attached to them. The serious Quakers likewise greatly blame them for their Conduct.

December 24 1755. To D. Barclay & Sons.

I understand Mr Hamilton has desired you to ship some small Arms &c., for the Use of the Province. As I know he gave the Owners of this Vessell an Expectation if she sailed as soon as any other, that he would desire you to give her the preference in taking said Guns on board. He is now out of Town being gone back to the Frontier of the Province. I therefore take the Freedom to mention that matter to you to request, in case the Vessell sails in time, that the Warlike Arms be put on board her.

March 3rd 1756. To D. Barclay & Sons.
Please to send me by first Opportunity
 2 Oz's of early Battersea Cabbage seed
 1 oz   Collyflower   do
 1 Oz   Roman Brocoli   do
 2 Oz of Sugarloaf Cabbage   do
 2 Oz of Coloured Carrot Seed
 4 Oz of the large Broadleaf Spinnage Seed
And pray let the Seeds be fresh & of this year for a Disappointment in my Garden is no small Mortification.

May 24 1756. To Mr John Wade in Carthagena.

As we were well informed that our Port was like to be shut up by an Embargo for three months; we therefore freighted the Ship, Charming Polly, Capt Dun, Master. * * * Mr Gibson further acquaints us that you incline to have a Vessel of about 110 Tuns built here on your Account, and has showed us your Letter to him on that Subject. As you would have her fitted, she will cost near One Third more than a Single Deck Vessel, built & fitted here in the usual manner, which Mr. Gibson says he told you would cost about 2500 Dollars. We were at first at some loss whether it would be advisable to set her up imagining you would expect her price would be much lower, than it would turn out in the End. But as he informs us it would be a Disappointment to you if she was not got ready; We have therefore ventured without Advise to have the Vessel built, and have employed our best Builder who will do the Work faithfully, and comply with your Directions in Mr. Gibson's Letter.

June 22, 1756. To Hon. Wm Nelson in Yorktown Va.
It will be, I presume, no News to tell you that Genl. Abercrombie with 2 Regiments are arrived at N. York. When the Residue with my Ld London are to be expected we are at a Loss, tho' it is said very shortly.

July 1 1757. To D Barclay & Sons.
I must likewise desire you to pay to Mr Ferdinando John Paris the Sum of £133. 0. 2d Sterling being the Ballance of his Account of Sollicitations &c. And to Mrs. Anna Irish the Sum of £50 Ster. being the Legacy left her by her Uncle, * * * Nathaniel Irish, dec'd.

July 30 1757. To D. Barclay & Sons.
The Bearer of this, Mr. Ralph Ashton is a Relation of Doctor Redman, and Served an apprenticeship with him. He comes over with an Intention to improve himself by tending the Hospitals. I am desired by the Doctor, who

writes to you by this Opportunity to give Mr Ashton a Credit for one Hundred pounds Sterling.

March 28 1758. To D. Barclay & Sons.

I wrote to Mr Hamilton a few days before he left Newyork, and desired he would get you to ship for me twelve half pieces of Cambrick & a piece of fine Lawn for my Family Use. And beg you would send to my Periwigmaker for a couple of Wigs to come by any Opportunity that may offer.

Nov 16th 1758. To D. Barclay & Son.

I have a little Boy, who teazes me to send for the Books undermentioned, which I beg you will be so kind as to buy & send me together with Warner's Ecclesiastical History for myself, if published. Books viz: Sir Charles Grandison; Clarissa Harlowe.

Feby 10 1759. To D. Barclay & Son.

I have received two Letters from One John Monkton, who was formerly Servant to One Mr. Charles Child of Guildford in Surry, and for Sometime waited on me in my Travels to France &c. complaining of being reduced to great Poverty. My Acquaintance & his was of no long standing, and is now an old Story; I well remember I satisfied him to his Content for any Services he did me; But as I think he was an honest man, and is, as he says, an Object of Charity, I desire if he be living, you will pay him on my Account Ten Guineas.

June 20 1759. To D. Barclay & Son.

I cannot omit mentioning to you that our Assembly have prevailed on the Governor to re-emit our paper Money, that we had before the War, for the Term of 16 years; which, as soon as the Army leaves us, will so far depreciate our Currency as to make Exchange rise from £150 (at which it is at present) to 200 or 300 p Cent especially as the Paper Money, we strike to carry on our Share of the War is not likely to be sunk at the periods mentioned in the Acts of Assembly. Should not this Law be disallowed by the King in Councill, the British Merchts, and all who have money owing to them will be great Sufferers, and all property rendered very insecure, and we shall be plunged into the same difficulties they have been in New England. * * * I must request, as soon as you are in Cash that you would buy for me £2000 Stg more Stock. It is true Interest is low with you, but the Principal will be safer than in a Country where the Currency is like to be reduced to less than half its value; I shall therefore endeavour to remit you what money I shall be able to call in, to guard, as far as in me lies, against the impending Ruin. I presume before this reaches you Mr. Hamilton will have left England; in case he should not, please to inform him, I think his sister seems now to be in a fair Way to be restored to her Health.

Oct. 18 1759. To D. Barclay & Son.

Mr Hamilton does not appear. I fear he has had a very blustering Voyage, as we lately have had many hard Gales of Wind. His presence is much wanted; for our venal Governer, and the party here are attacking every Right of Government, by the Laws they are making.

Feby 9 1760. To D. Barclay & Sons.

I need not tell you that Mr Hamilton is arrived. His Affairs hitherto have a pleasing Aspect, his accepting the Government being very agreeable to the best people of our Province ; I hope they will continue in this way ; But as we have a grumbling Hive, there is no certainty that an honest, candid Administration will be satisfactory to our politicians. We have a man of Honor to deal with now; we before had a poor mercenary Creature that was justly despised by all good men among us.

March 10 1760.   To D. Barclay & Sons.

Since writing my last letter, my Son John, who is now of Age, having an Inclination to see a little of the World, is about to take a Voyage to Leghorn, and proposes to stay a few Months in Italy, and from thence to come down the Streights & take his Passage from Lisbon or some other Port to London. I should take it as a particular Favor, if you would procure Letters of Credit & Recommendation to some Gentlemen at Leghorn, Naples, Genoa, Rome & Milan.

When I travelled, I found that these letters of Credence were of great Use to me, as they procured me acquaintance in every place I came to.

He is accompanied by a young Gentleman, a Relation of mine, Mr Joseph Shippen, who has been an Officer in our provincials ever since the war, was Major of Brigade to General Forbes, and last year Lieut Colonel in one of the Province Regiments ; he is a very sober, virtuous, sensible young man, and I think my Son happy in such a Companion.

My Son has hitherto proved a virtuous well inclined Lad, and have not perceived the least Turn to Vice in him, I have not therefore limited him as to his Expence, but have earnestly recommended Frugality. I wish when you write to your Friends, you would be pleased to mention in your Letters Colonel Shippen.

The Betty Sally * * * is a Letter of Marque and carries 12 Carriage Guns & 20 Men.

Phila. 5th April 1760.

Gentlemen:

Your very agreeable Favor of the 26th of October by Way of New York, and Copy of the same from London, in which you are so good as to propose a Renewal of our Correspondence, gave me great pleasure.

As I have had the Honor to be Chief Justice of this Prov'nce for near ten years past, I have, in a great Measure, declined all trade; But, agreeable to your desire, I mentioned the Contents of your Letter, to some of my Friends, particularly the encouraging prices of Sugar at present at your Market. A Number of us sent three Ships the last year of the late War laden with Sugars. The precipitate fall of the prices, at that Time, made us great Sufferers; however, upon so good a prospect, as you mention, some of my friends here resolved to make a Trial; among the rest my Son John, whom I have brought up to Business and a Relation of mine, Mr. Joseph Shippen, who had both a mind to see Italy, with some other Gentlemen agreed to load the Vessel by which this comes, & put her under the care of Mr. Shippen & my Son, to whom I have recommended to put the Concern into your Hands, which they will undoubtedly do, in case they arrive safe.

Our Flag of Truce trade has lately met with an Interruption, a great part of them, near fifteen Sail being taken & carried into Jamaica, Providence &c. Had they arrived safe we should have had French Sugars in plenty; and I could, I am persuaded, have prevailed on some of my Friends here to have sent some of their Vessels to your address, of which, I still do not despair, should any number arrive safe, which, I presume will be the Case. I have a Sort of Promise from Mr. Gibson a Relation of my Wife's, who has a Vessel sailed for Holland last Fall, the Master of which has Orders to proceed to Monto Christi, and there to take in a Cargo of white Sugars for this port; that he will, upon the Vessel's Arrival, if the War continues address her to you.

Mr. Shippen & my Son propose chiefly by this Voyage to have the pleasure of visiting the different parts of Italy; I must request therefore the favor of you to procure them Letters of Recommendation and Credit to the several Towns they shall go through. I have wrote to my Friends at London likewise to this purpose, who, I doubt not procure such for them. I received part of my Education at Clarehall in Cambridge, at which time Mr. Horatio Man, the present Resident at Florence, was then a Fellow Student; upon the Strength of which I have ventured depending on his Character for Humanity & Kindness to his Countrymen, to write to him on Mr. Shippen's & my Son's Behalf, to which, I should be much obliged to you, if you would add yours & some of your Friend's Weight.

Mr. Shippen has been an Officer in our provincial Troops for four or five years past, was Brigade Major to General Forbes at the taking of Fort Du Quesne, and served as Lieut. Colonel last Campaign under General Stanwix. He is a very ingenious virtuous young man, and I think myself happy in my Son's having such a Companion. I am fearful, however, he will soon lose him, except there should be a peace, as he intends to become a Trader, to which he was in part bred, and is desirous of going to Alicant & Malaga in order to load the Vessel with Wine & Brandy & other things, the Produce of Spain. I have told him that part of the Business can be as well done in his Absence, by your writing to your Correspondents to get such things as are wanted ready again the Vessel comes down; however, in case he should go down with the Vessel, I am in hopes he will return while my Son continues at Florence.

As Sundry of the Owners will give Orders for purchasing of some Silks & other things for their Family's Use, I presume you can procure them, while the Ship stays, from Genoa, as Sundry Articles cannot be purchased so cheap, or so good in kind with you. I beg you would be so kind as to let Parmesan Cheese be rich & mild, as I am very fond of what is good of that kind of Cheese, and that the other things that are for family Consumption be well chosen. The small Gorgona Anchovies, I think, are the most esteemed.

In this Vessel comes a passenger, Mr. West, a young ingenious Painter of this City, who is desirous to improve himself in that Science, by visiting Florence & Rome; but being unacquainted how to have his Money remitted has lodged with me One hundred pounds Sterling, which I shall remit to Messrs David Barclay & Sons upon his Account: I beg therefore you would give him a Credit for that Sum and take his Bills for the Amount; and should be further obliged to you for any kindness you show him, as he has among us the Character of a very deserving young man. I am in hopes I shall have more Opportunities of writing to you this Summer.

In the mean time conclude with assuring you that I am
Your most Obedt. Humble Servt.
                                            W. Allen.
To
   Messrs Jackson & Rutherford,
       Merch.ts. in Leghorn ; per Mr. John Allen in ye
Ship Betty Sally, Capt. Sneed.

April 16 1760. D. Barclay & Sons.

My Son sailed out of our Capes the 12th of this Inst. * * * You have inclosed William Plumsted & David Franks Bill * * * for £101 6s. 2d. Sterl. which I am desired by Mr. Benjamin West to remit to you, and and which you will be pleased to carry to his Credit when received. * * * He is a young Painter that goes Passenger in the Ship with my Son in order to improve himself in the Science of painting, and lodges the money with you, in order to answer his Expenses, whilst in Italy.

May 19 1760. To Jackson & Rutherford at Leghorn.

I desire you would procure for me from Genoa, six pieces of good black Paduasoy without any selvage, being for Mourning Scarfs, much used at Buryings in this Country. The Selvage of a different Colour, which is often the case of Italian Silks renders them unfit for this Use. * * *

Captain Rutherford who married a lady at New York, has had a Wind-fall, his Wife's Mother, Mrs Alexander being lately deceased, by which one Sixth part of her Estate Real & Personal comes to Mrs Rutherford. Various are the Accounts of the Amount of her share; in my Opinion, it will be worth between £15,000 and

£20,000 Sterling; there being a very great Estate in Lands and a considerable personal one. * * *

I have lately had the Misfortune to lose my good ancient Mother, and last week, died my much loved Wife, which has Shocked me to a great degree.

October 6 1760. To John Griffiths, jr. Caerleon Mills Monmouthshire.

Our Iron Masters here think three Tons, a Week, may be made at each Finery; and it has been done here in one Forge, have never exceeded Seven Tons in the Chafery, with a Hammer to itself: It will therefore be an Improvement, if your People can draw two Tons more.

You may depend upon it that this is one of the best poor Man's Country in the World, and agrees very well with English Constitutions.

Oct 20 1760. To D. Barclay & Sons.

I have received your very agreeable Favour * * advising me of your having purchased £1500 more Stock for me in the 3 p Cent consolidated Annuities @ 82⅜ p Cent. for which with Brokg you debit me £1245.

I have some distant thoughts in case there should be a Peace this Winter, of coming to London, & bringing with me two of my Sons, whom I intend to place in the Temple, and think to spend a Winter in England, & return in the Spring. * * *

I must request you would be so good as to get a Mourning Ring made for our Governor of five Guineas value, on Account of his Sister's Death. I had in the time of my great distress, desired Mr. Turner to mention this to you, but I fear he has omitted it. "Margaret Allen; died the 12th May 1760, aged 51."

March 25 1761. To D. Barclay & Sons.

I have not had a line from him (John Allen) since he left Leghorn to go his Tour. The December Pacquet, I understand is taken, and the Letter you forwarded by Bolitho miscarried. I inclose you one to him, which I beg you would be so good as to deliver, and that you would be pleased to afford him your favour, & Countenance during his stay in England.

I am very much obliged to you for the kind Regards you were pleased to express on my coming to England, in which I was fully determined had there been a peace. I have always had a sincere Friendship for your good Family; and have long experienced the Goodness and Worth of your David Barclay the Elder; and tho' we have the Atlantick between us, I have & always shall esteem him as one of my worthiest Friends.

March 25 1761. To John Griffiths.

Our manager, Mr. Hackett, says the new Iron we make yields so well that less than 26 cwt. of Pigs will make a Ton of Bar. * * * Since we have wrote you, we have finished our small Blast and from the first Day of September to the first of December our Furnace produced 332 Tons of Pig metal, which was beyond our most sanguine expectations. * * * Water & Wood we never can want, indeed we want nothing but good Workmen; tho' we reckon we have some of the best this Country affords; who say that Three Tons of Ankongs a week may be made. * * * our Workmen have, for a Trial, made more than that Quantity, but it remains a Mystery to them, how Nine Tuns can be drawn at a Chafery. * * * We are content that you bring with you a pair of Forge Bellows, but believe those we have being made of Wood, willl answer as well, if not better, and will last twenty years. No other than Wooden Bellows are now used among us either at our Furnaces or Forges, and by experience we find that the Blast from them is much better than those made of Leather, for which reason they are universally disused. A German introduced the Wooden Bellows among us; and by constructing them at ye different Iron Works, has made a pretty good Fortune;—We may call it such, for he has now a Forge of his own and rents a Furnace. * * * Some considerable Fortunes have been made by Iron Works with us, and our present Manager, is become an Owner with us in our New Works; and, if he lives, will be a rich man.

July 20 1751. To Francis J. Tysson, Esq. Upper Brooke St.

Old Mr. Jonathan Dickinson had a grant from the Proprietary Agents for twenty Acres of low Ground upon Condition, I am told, of draining & improving the same, which he did not live, or neglected to accomplish. The Title therefore to that is precarious and depends I presume, on the Proprietaries for Confirmation; which old Mr. Logan, nor I could obtain; you may be informed more particularly of the Circumstances of that Affair of his Son, if he has not left England.

July 20 1761. To D. Barclay & Sons.

This comes by my two Sons Andrew & James whom I send to England, in order to study the Law in the Temple. I had, as I wrote you thoughts of accompanying them, had peace taken place but I must delay my Voyage till that Event happens, which I presume & hope will be within the Compass of this year. In the mean time I request you would be so good as to afford them your Countenance, Friendship, & advice. I spent six years at one time, in England, and am very sensible they are to go thro' a fiery Trial. The many Temptations youths are exposed to in your City, and the Vice & Luxury that is too predominant, make me very anxious on their Account. I have taken the greatest care in my power of their Education hitherto, and in forming their Minds to Virtue. And as yet their conduct has been such as rather to give me Pleasure than Pain; but they are now embarking in a new Scene: They will be, in a great Measure, left to themselves, remote from me their Parent, & from their very affectionate Uncle, Governor Hamilton, who seems greatly interested in their Welfare, and to whose kind lessons and Example they are much indebted.

I must further beg you would be so good as to supply them with Money for their Expenses; which I would not chuse should exceed two hundred pounds a year, for each of them, exclusive of Books, and the first fitting them with Clothes & a few other necessities.

Among other lessons I have taught them that of Frugality, & Oeconomy has been much pressed upon them, without which their Studies will be neglected, and there will be danger of their plunging into Vice.

I think they are honest Lads, and far from being deficient in a Capacity to acquire Knowledge, of rather more Vivacity, & higher Spirits than their Brother John, particularly Andrew, whose Temper seems rather too quick, of which I have frequently cautioned him.

I would have them take Chambers in the Temple, in the procuring of which their Uncle's Friends may be able to advise them, he having wrote to some of them for their friendly Countenance and Advice.

I am very sensible of the Trouble I am like to give you, and must depend upon your goodness and particularly on the long Friendship I have had the pleasure to support with your Mr David Barclay the Elder, to excuse the Freedom I take, in recommending the youths to your care, and at the same time beg leave to return you my sincere thanks, for your kindness to my eldest Son, John, to whom I have wrote that I would have him leave England sometime next Winter or Spring, so as to be here in April, or May next; For I think it will be time to set himself down to business, tho' everything is so overdone, that it is difficult now among us, how to employ Money to advantage in the trading way.

I have drawn on you for twenty one pounds Sterling * * * being for my two Son's passages.

Aug 10 1761. To D. Barclay & Sons.

I have not time at present to write to my Son John; But beg you would tell him that I have received his Letter by the Pacquet, and that I approve of his advancing the £60 to Mr West; and that his Uncle & I have agreed to advance him £100 more, which additional Snm I desire he would remit Mr West as soon as possible, which I beg you would be so kind as to pay to my Son, or Mr West's Order. From all Accounts he is like to turn out a very extraordinary person in the Painting Way, and it is a pity such a Genius should be cramped for want of a little Cash.

Sept 11 1761. To D. Barclay & Sons.

I desire you would purchase as much more Stock, as will make what you have already bought for me £8000. Pray be so kind as to tell my Son John, to whom I have not time to write, that at his Uncle's Instance I am desirous he should buy for his Sister Nancy, as much of a well fancied Brocade as will make his Sister a Suit of Clothes.

December 3rd 1761. Wm Nelson, Yorktown Va.

Your Neighbour Mr Tabb informed me that Mountain Wine would sell with you. My Son John * * * being concerned in a Cargo of Sugar * * * up the Streights; Upon the Return of the Vessel, the Master was ordered to call at Malaga to take in a parcel of Wines; part of which, being fifty Quarter Casks I take the Freedom to request you would be pleased to sell, for the most they will yield with you.

I have shipped them in a Shallop belonging to Mr Waters, a relation of my deceased Wife's; his Master has signed a Bill of Lading, which you have herewith inclosed, to deliver the Wine to you. As the Vessell is a small Coaster, and has other things to deliver in Somerset County, for Mr Waters, she has not cleared out from our Custom-House, it not being usual for these small Coasters. I hope therefore you will prevent any Trouble to the Master from our mutual Friend Mr Ambler, or any other person. * * * It gave me no small Concern when I returned from the Back Country where I had been trying some Criminals, to find that I had missed the pleasure of paying my Regards to your Son, who, it seems passed through this town in my absence.

December 21st 1761. To D. Barclay & Sons.

I am apt to think a Peace, will as you formerly mentioned to me make them produce good Interest for money in the end. Should that event happen, as I am still inclined to see England once more, I shall take a trip over & see my old Friends, and examine how my young Templers are going on.

Feby 15. 1762. To D. Barclay & Sons.
Give me leave to acknowledge your kindness & Civility to my Sons, but as I have long experienced many Signal Instances of your Friendship, I shall not dwell on this Subject.

Andrew & James are soliciting me very hard for an Increase of their Allowance; and their Uncle is of Opinion that I should do it.

I must therefore intreat you to increase the same £50 a year to each of them. Though I fear it will enable them to have more Avocations from their real Business, the Study of the Law. If it should have that effect, it would be very vexatious to me. I should be much obliged to you, if you would be so kind as to give me any Information you may receive how they spend their Time, and whether the large Expense I am at will be counter-waited by their good Behaviour and Dilligence.

Your Friend, our Governor has hitherto, had an easy and peaceable Administration, our late Factioneers having much less weight in the Assembly than formerly; what Effect their Chief, Mr Franklin's Return among them may produce, must be left to time. One would fain hope his almost insatiable ambition is pretty near Satisfied by his parading about England &c. at the province's Expense for these five years past, which now appears in a different Light to our patriots than formerly especially, as he has already stayed near two years longer; than they expected; a sample of which is their refusing to put the Second Sum received from the Crown into his Hands—a matter to which I did not a little contribute.

April 12 1762.   To D. Barclay & Sons.

I find London is a very expensive place ; and that my Sons are like to spend me a good deal of more Money than I expected; however I must be content ; the more they spend now, the less they will have to receive, when I go off the Stage.

I shall not grudge the expense in case they make good Use of their Time. I am content, as I wrote you before that my Sons Andrew and James should spend £250 each besides their Books, and beyond that I should not chuse they should go : however, in case any unforseen matter should happen, I shall leave it to your Discretion to supply them with what may be absolutely necessary, and be quite satisfied with what you do. But I must at the same time give my Opinion that more than £250 will do them more harm I fear, than good, and furnish them only with too many Avocations from their Studies. * * * Pray be so good as to tell James, I have received no Letter by the Pacquet from him, which does not please me, of which please to inform him. I am told they keep good Company, which I much approve of ; But I have told them much precious Time as well as Money may be spent if they are too often in even good Company. I depend on your Goodness to excuse the Trouble I give you about my Children ; But the Anxiety of a parent, I hope, will induce you to make allowances.

June 29 1762.   A. Stuart to D. Barclay & Son.

This serves to inform you that Mr. Allen * * * has been for a fortnight past in Easton attending an Indian Treaty, where he is like to remain a few days longer, as he is not quite recovered from a Smart Fit of the Gout he was there seized with.

October 10 1762. To D. Barclay & Sons.

I have received your letter of the 20th of May, by my Son John, whose long stay in Bristol made me very apprehensive he was taken, or lost; his safe arrival has given me great pleasure, and his Uncle and I, are both well pleased with him, as he seems a good deal improved. He expresses a high sense of your Goodness and Civilities to him, for which I beg leave to return you my most cordial Thanks, and request the Continuance of your kindness & Friendship to his Brothers. I duly note what you were pleased to mention about an Increase in their Allowance, upon which subject I have received a couple of Letters from Jemmy, to which have given him an Answer.

Upon consulting their Uncle, who is always rather too indulgent to them, he joins with me in Opinion that their Allowance ought not to be increased, only in respect to their Chamber Rent, which I request you will give them money to pay to commence from the Beginning of their entering them.

Mr Hamilton & I have employed Mr West to copy for us a Number of the best Pictures in Italy, where he has been very much indisposed, and his Sickness been so expensive to him that he cannot continue there without Cash be remitted to him. I have already supplied him with £150 Sterling. Mr Hamilton has promised to give me a Bill of Exchange for the like Sum in order to put the young Fellow in Cash. I must therefore desire you would immediately advise Messrs Jackson & Rutherford of Leghorn that you will honor their Bills for any Sum not exceeding £150 on Mr West's Account, and carry the same when paid to my Debit. We have such an **extraordinary** Account of Mr West's Genius in the painting Way that we venture to afford him these Supplies, and for his Incouragement to take it out in Copies.

October 30 1762. To D. Barclay & Sons.
As I have lately wrote fully to my Sons, I beg only you will tell them we are all well and have escaped a Sickness, that for some time, was alarming, being a Species of the Yellow Fever. The Town is at present clear of that infectious Disease.

December 4 1762. To Wm Hopkins, Paul's Church Yard, London.
I herewith inclose you a Bill of Lading for a Box containing 104 Sorts of the Seeds of the Forest Trees and Shrubs &c of this Country for my Lord Gage.

December 4 1762. To D. Barclay & Sons.
I should have chose to have made you further Remittances in the same specie, but hear that the Quantity taken in the Hermione has greatly reduced the price of Silver, and the Reduction of the Havannah will, no doubt, still keep it down, and perhaps lower it still more, so that probably it will be no advantageous Remittance. I am glad to find that the Stocks have risen, but by what you write, and by other advices, a peace is not far off, which makes it not adviseable to buy in any more Stock; I shall therefore decline any further thoughts of increasing my Interest in that way.

Should that desirable Event of a Peace happen, I have still some thoughts of taking a Trip to England, tho' it begins to be late in Life for me to be travelling, having now and then some Attacks of the Gout; tho', in other Respects, I retain a great Share of Health. I spent a good part of my Youth in England, which makes me have an earnest desire, once more, to revisit it, and I firmly believe I shall, tho' the Governor and some other of my friends laugh when I talk of it.

I wrote you so fully in relation to my Son's Allowance for their Support, that I think it unnecessary to say any thing further upon that Head at present. If I come over, I shall regulate all that matter and prevent you from any further Trouble from their Solicitations on that Head. I would cheerfully let them have as much money as I think will do them good; but not so much as would give them too many Avocations from their Studies.

My Son John is returned and his Behaviour gives me pleasure. Tho' he has spent me some Cash, yet it seems that he has had the advantage of seeing the World & keeping good Company. When I mention him give me leave to acquaint you that he has by this Opportunity sent some of his Friends three Boxes of the Seeds of the Forest Trees & Shrubs of this Country, which I beg you would be so good as to take care of and deliver to John Mytton, Edward Sonthwell and Thomas Wynn, Esq. when they call for them.

Philadelphia 12 Dec 1762. Mr Thos Simpson.

I do not know that any thing gave me more uneasiness than the Mishap of the Lands first Surveyed. I was impowered by your Father to survey, and locate the Rights of Land I purchased for him whilst I was in England. Those in this Province, after the Rights were located, I bought of him, and gave him twenty-five pounds more than the whole cost him, viz the Third of Propriety in West New Jersey and fifteen hundred Acres in Pennsylvania. With regard to a Third of a propriety, being upwards of 6000 Acres, I employed a person, Mr

John Budd, who was always esteemed an honest Man, and well acquainted with with the Jerseys, where he lived, and employed by Mr Penn's Family to take up large Quantities of Land for them, to survey the Land your Father was entitled to, and gave him very particular Directions to chuse out the best Spots that were to be had, and to have the Surveys regularly recorded in the proper Offices, which he accordingly did, and I sent copies of the said Surveys to your good Father. The Information I had from the person employed, and from many others, was, that the Lands were very good, and that, in time they would come to be of great value, tho' then they were remote from the Inhabitants.

About seven, or eight years since upon examining the the Lines that divide East & West Jersey, by the Proprietors of both Divisions, it was found that the Lands Surveyed for Mr. Simpson were in East Jersey, whereas they should have been surveyed in West Jersey. Upon which those that had rights to East Jersey Lands surveyed them for their own use, as if they had been vacant, which has deprived the Estate of any Benefit from the former Location, and has rendered that Interest of little Value, there being now left only the Right of taking up the Land in West Jersey, where there are no Vacancies except miserable Barrens.

This unhappy Case was not the Lot of your Family only, but also happened to a very great Number of other People many of which resided at, or near the Places and Tracts of Land they had taken up, and consequently were less liable to be mistaken in the Bounds of the two Divisions.

Some hundred thousand Acres of Land either have been totally lost to the Owners of them, or they have been obliged to buy Rights to East Jersey Lands, and to survey & return them anew to the East Jersey Offices. When this matter was discovered East Jersey Rights rose in value treble what they were before, on account of the number of people that wanted to save their Land. The Proprietors of East Jersey were just enough by proclamation to give all the unhappy Sufferers two years Time to buy Eastern Rights to cover their former Surveys. Sundry people as I said before, made use of that Opportunity, whereas many others on account of the high price of Eastern Rights, chose rather to lose their Lands than by those Rights.

Your Father's Lands were good, and had he been living, I would have apprised him of this matter, and taken his directions; But as the affairs of the Family were situated, I did not think it advisable to lay out the sum of £2000 Sterling, which would Scarce have been Sufficient to save the Lands, especially as they would have been liable to have been sold for the benefit of his Creditors, and I perhaps puzzled to have got the money again in such an intricate affair. * * * Your Father's Lands there (East Jersey) are now in the possession of persons who, after the two years were elapsed, had them surveyed to their own use as East Jersey Lands.

March 7th 1763. To D. Barclay & Sons.

My Sons' Expenses I think to be more than I am willing they should continue to spend; I am sure they are more, by near one half, than I was allowed, and I lived handsomely, and kept as good Company as they can do, and never left any Trades Men's Bills unpaid.

As I have, by Bolitho, mentioned to you what I was willing to allow them, after a Consultation with their Uncle, I need not say any thing further on this Head, only that in what you have hitherto exceeded my Limits with regard to their Expenses, as I am confident you have done it for the best; I do cheerfully agree to it. I am very sensible of the Trouble you must have from the Solicitations of my Youngsters, and reckon myself much obliged to you for your many Acts of kindness extended to them, of which shall always retain a grateful Sense.

As I propose coming over in Budden, I shall, as I wrote you, settle all matters with my Boys about their Allowance, at the same time have an Opportunity of paying my regards to you. Mr Alexander Barclay proposed to me to send his Son & to put him under my Care during the Voyage, which I readily agreed to, and hope to deliver him safe into the Hands of you his Relations. * * * I flatter myself with the Pleasure of seeing you Sometime in June.

Sept 25 1764. To D. Barclay & Sons.

But upon examining the Same, (the Account) I find my Son's Expenses exceed much any thing I could have imagined ; it was full time to put an end to it ; I hope they will turn their Thoughts to Business, and think of getting money for their future Subsistence, and become useful to themselves, and their Country.

Our People's Thoughts are employed entirely upon the approaching Elections, both Sides seem confident of Success; but from what I hear, there will be a change of the Members. I shall not intermeddle, nor be in the Town the day of the Election ; I hope the Peace will be preserved : yet, from the mutual Heats, it is to be feared there will be warm work. The Serious Friends seem to be dissatisfied with the Intention to change the Government, and very probably, Mr Hunt's advice may have weight with such ; The younger folks are, I think, too much under the Influence of that Disturber of the Peace, Franklin, & his Creatures.

Upon a motion of mine in the House, the Committee of Correspondency were ordered to lay before the Members, their Letter to Mr. Jackson relative to the Petition to the King for a Change of Government, which being produced, I had almost lost my usual patience, for it contained many Scandalous Reflections upon the Judges and Magistracy, as if Justice could not be obtained in the Province, owing to the Proprietary Influence, and their being appointed by them. I told them this was a poor Return for our long & faithful Services; that we never had desired our Office, but served in them for no lucrative Motives, but from a Sense of Duty; that we never had, nor ever would be under any Influence but that of Justice, and I defied them to point out one Instance to the contrary ; That I had served the Public for thirty-five years in Courts of Justice, and that I did not remember two Proprietary Law Suits ; That their Letter contained many infamous Falsehoods, which I was ready to make out. I was answered that they never intended to reflect on us; That they owned we were honest men, but that bad Men might come after us, and that, tho' the Proprietors brought no Actions hitherto, they might bring 10,000. They were told that would be owing to the Injustice of those who with-held their due from them ; that it was time to complain when they suffered any wrong. The whole of these Clamours are owing to the Malice of Franklin & Galloway, who have a great deal to answer for plunging the Province into Confusion.

I hope, & believe their reign is short, and am persuaded all their Efforts for further Mischief will be, in a great measure prevented in time to come, whatever way the next Elections are determined, for the People begin to open their Eyes daily, and they would scarce be so hardy as to attempt the Same Measures again. My coming in, and the News I brought, has made them much down in the Mouth, and several violent measures have already, in the House of Assembly, been rendered abortive; Tho' it is composed chiefly of Franklin's Creatures, and such as have been hitherto deluded. So much for Politicks.

* * * I have likewise taken the freedom to inclose a Letter to that worthy Patriot, Mr. Pitt, and to send a Box of Pine Buds for him, directed to your care, which please to send to him. I have not the Honor of being known to him, but, as I hear he is much troubled with the Gout, I have taken the freedom to recommend the Use of them, to him.

You mention some Proposal made to me when at Portsmouth, which I do not recollect: Matters must subside before a Bank can take place, which, I hope, will not be long. Pray request your Mr John Barclay, to inform me whether his friend, Sir John Fielding, has taken any Steps to recover my Black Girl, or whether there is any Account of her

My Daughters desire their Compliments to you, and request you would discharge Mrs Lamar's Account with them, and that you would send them a couple of Pair of fashionable Paste-Buckles, and a Leather Hunting-woman's Saddle, being for my Daughter Margaret, who, I presume, would be in the Fashion, when she rides.

Philada 25 Septr 1764.

Sir;

Tho' I have not the Honor of being known to you, yet I am no Stranger to your eminent & virtuous Character, nor to the great Service you have rendered your Country.

We have greatly partook of your Salutary Councils in this part of the World ; whilst you was in the Ministry, you revived our drooping Spirits; and to you it is in a great measure owing that our Properties are Secure, and an insolent Enemy that threatened to drive us into the Sea, were themselves conquered. We should be the most ungrateful of men did we not love & highly respect so worthy a Patriot. This we all do with great Sincerity of Heart, and pray God your precious Life may long be preserved, and that your Health may enable you to render your Country still further Service.

I am one who have for fourteen years past been afflicted with the Gout ; and as I perceive by the public papers you are visited with that malady, I have taken the freedom to send you some of the Pine Buds, which, being made into a Tea, have been of infinite Service to me & many others in this part of the World. It is the Tar-Water, without the heating Quality, and has many other Vertues superadded to that Remedy ; it is perfectly innocent, is an alterative, & must be used for a length of time. I have taken it pretty constantly for my Breakfast, for these Seven years past. Before I used it, I had two or three fits of the Gout every year, but now have it only once in eighteen Months, & the Fits but very Light. It will not cure the Gout, but will render it less frequent, & the fits easy. It is much esteemed by all the Physicians in our parts, is prescribed in Gouty, Rheumatic, & Asmahtic Cases, for all Disorders in the Breast ; As it is vastly diuretic, it is likewise very useful in the Gravel.

I am lately returned to my Native Country from England, where I Spent a twelve-month, and carried over with me about fifty weight, which I distributed to sundry Physicians & other Gentlemen. The Physicians had a high Opinion of it, particularly Dr Fothergil. I gave some of it to the present Ld Chancellor, & to my Ld Ellebank, & to sundry Gentlemen at the Club at Saunders, of which place I was a Member. If you will be pleased to get any of your Friends to enquire of the Gentlemen I have named, you will be informed of its Qualities I never knew it fail of rendering Service to such persons as have used it for any time. It helps Digestion, promotes an Appetite, and inclines greatly to Sleep; It is the finest preparation of Turpentine, and I do not know that it can be injurious to any person, but such as are afflicted with the Stone, to whom it may possibly give pain by its being rather too forcing. I gave some of it to Mr. Penn, the Proprietor of Pennsylvania, and as he had the largest Quantity, he no doubt gave some of it to others, and can inform you what Effects it had upon such as made use of it. The Quantity I have sent will be sufficient for a year or two. If by any means I can be acquainted that you receive Benefit by the Buds, I will yearly supply you with any Quantity. They are gathered in this Climate between the 20th Feby & 20th March. In order to receive the more immediate Benefit, it would be best, for a couple of Months to take about a pint of the Tea twice a day, afterwards once a day will be Sufficient,—indeed the Tea may be omitted now & then for a week or two; But I rarely miss having it for my Breakfast, as by long use it is pleasanter to me than any other kind of Tea.

As I have no other Motive for taking this Freedom, but a desire to contribute all in my power towards your Health & Ease, I beg therefore you would so good as to

excuse, & make the proper Allowance for the Zeal & Affection of,
  Sir,
    Your Most Obedt Humble Servant
      William Allen.
To
 The Rt Hon.ble
  Wm. Pitt, Esq.
   London.

Oct 24 1764. To Rob. Davis, Bookseller in Piccadilly.
 I have sent you two Bushels of Timothy Grass Seed, for Mr. Roaque, from whom please to receive the Cost of the same being £3. 0. 6d Stg. The demand for that Seed has been so great, I believe chiefly for England, that it has risen to an enormous price. I should be glad you would continue to send me the Magazines, at least the two Sorts you lately sent, and any curious Pamphlets, or Books; and you may depend whenever you send me your Accounts, that I will give you Orders on Messrs Barclay in Cheapside to pay off the same.
 I have been speaking to an honest careful man here to send you next Summer a large Quantity of the Pine Buds; and I tell him that you & he are to be joint Sharers in what Profits may arise upon the Sale of them. If this proposal is agreeable to you, it will be an encouragement to the man, whose name is James Alexander; he is one of our curious Botanists, and Supplies many of the Nobility with Seeds of the Trees & Shrubs of America. As the Buds cannot be gathered till March next, you will have time to consider whether the Man's Terms are agreeable to you; Should you come into this proposal I believe Alexander will send you a large

Quantity, perhaps a couple of Thousand Weight, or if he cannot supply that Quantity, some others may on the same Terms.

I have an account that my Ld Chancellor, and my Ld Chief-Justice Pratt have both received considerable Benefit since I left England, by the Use of them, which has emboldened me to send about three Gallons of them to that worthy Patriot, Mr. Pitt, out of my own Stock gathered last Spring.

Oct 24 1764.   To D. Barclay & Sons.

You have Copies of my Letters to Mr. Penn & Mr Jackson which will apprise you with the State of Affairs in the Province.

Franklin has still so great hold of the Country Members that he is like to be appointed joint Agent with Mr. Jackson, which, I believe, will be done this Evening.

The Serious Friends at length begin to be alarmed, but unhappily for the Province they seem to have as little weight with the Members of the Counties of Bucks & Chester, who with a few others compose a Majority of the House, as any other sober persons.

I wish your Mr David Barclay junior would inform my Ld Hide what Sort of a man Franklin is; as you are so well acquainted with his Character I need not mention it.

November 20 1764.   To D. Barclay & Sons.

This comes by our worthy Friend Mr. Hamilton, who is advised by our Physicians, again to visit London on account of a Disorder that he has on his Nose, which, they are somewhat apprehensive may turn to a Cancer, as his Mother & Sister were afflicted with that Malady; all his Friends have concurred with the Doctors in persuading him to take the Voyage. He will, with you, have the Assistance of the most able Physicians & Surgeons—God grant that he may meet with Relief, and that he may return in good Health among his Friends again. He is well acquainted with all Occurrences here, so that it is needless for me to say much upon these matters: Only, thus far let me tell you, that I took all the pains in my power to reconcile our Differences, but had not so much Success as I could wish: I have hereby drawn on me the Resentment of the contentious, particularly of the grand Incendiary, Franklin, who, the day before he left Town, published a very abusive paper, chiefly levelled against me, in which he takes Notice of a Letter of yours to Abel James, insinuating that I had been impowered by the Proprs. to settle ye Disputes between them & the People; and that I had neglected so to do; that I had wrote traiterous papers, and distributed them among the Dutch; whereas, in truth, I never wrote any paper, nor even read any of the Scurrilous Papers published on each Side, did not even go out the day of Election, nor give my vote. The Occasion of the base fellow's Malice at this Time against me, I presume, was owing to his hearing that a great many people came to consult me what part they had best act in the then ensuing Election, and that I had advised them against a Change of Government, & consequently to vote against the Authors of that attempt, which he imagines was the Occasion of his losing his Election. Indeed one of his partizans told me that if I had remained in England they would have carried their Election by 500 Votes. He has filled his papers with Sundry other infamous Falsehoods. He is so bad a man that I hope he will not receive any Countenance from honest Men in England. John Hunt, with whom I have conversed here, will, no doubt inform his Friends of the Disposition & Temper of our people here; I am told he laboured to bring them to another Mind, &, I believe prevailed on sundry of the serious People, but the Bulk had suffered themselves to be so far inflamed that they were not easily to be reclaimed; I am, however, not without hopes these Matters will subside, as the Heads of the Faction are removed out of the Assembly, and the City & County of Philadelphia are, in a great Measure, rescued out of their Hands, and it is expected their Creatures will probably lose their Elections the next year in the other Counties, as many people are daily convinced of their bad Designs, and if that should happen peace would be restored among us,—which God grant. For which Reasons I would fain hope the Proprietors would be induced to keep the Government. I know Mr Hamilton has so long experienced our People's factious Dispositions, that he used to think it would be best to give them up to the Crown. His Friends here have requested him not to advise such a measure, and I entreat you would concur with me in persuading him to use his Interest with the proprietary Family not to part with the Rights of Government, & for their Incouragement, I can say they never had a greater Number of Warm Friends than at present, for the fear of losing our Charter Rights, which it is impossible we should keep under the Crown (or at least the most valuable of them) makes people here much attached to them, and it seems a Sort of Madness in your Friends not to be in the same Disposition; But I hope they will change their Sentiments & see their true Interest, which is not so like effected by anything so soon as by the wholesome advice of Friends in England. * * *

I desire if your Cooper thinks it (a pipe of Wine) very good, and not otherwise, to let Colonel Barre have it, I having promised to send a pipe to him to be divided between my Ld Shellborn and him, in return for some presents he made me. * * *

No doubt you will hear fully of the low Ebb of Trade, which is distressed exceedingly; even the Intercourse between here & New Jersey is, in a great Measure interrupted, which was carried on in Flats & small Boats, and the Produce of the Western part of that Colony shipped off from this City, But now, one of those poor fellows cannot take in a few Staves, or Pig Iron, or Bar Iron, or Tar &c., but they must go thirty or forty Miles, or more to give Bond, the Charge of which & his travelling, make the Burthen intollerable.

It never was the Intention of the Legislature at home to destroy this little River-Trade, which is carried on in a kind of Market Boats, but their Regulations were only for Sea Vessels. This is a general Complaint all over the Continent; Such Measures will soon make us poor, but our Creditors in England will suffer with us. We must learn Frugality and make all our necessaries ourselves, for we shall soon not be able to get them any other way, as our Money is gone, and our Credit will soon be at on end.

December 19, 1764. To D. Barclay & Sons.

I hope this will find our mutual Friend, Mr Hamilton, safe arrived in good health. His Friends here are very desirous that he would exert himself in detecting the vile aspersions, which that artful man lately gone from hence will throw upon the good people here, who would soon be at peace, & be sensible of their own Happiness under our excellent Constitution, was it not for him, & his Adherents, who delight to fish in troubled Waters.

Should the Stocks take a favorable Turn, I should be pleased to have mine sold, but leave that to your better Judgment, for as you are on the Spot, you can guess whether they are like to rise or fall; if there is no prospect of their advancing, the sooner you sell them the better, for I can make a better Interest of my money here; And as our Money is yearly sinking, it will, as it grows less, improve in value; But, tho' our Paper Money, owing to its Scarcity, may do so, yet our Real Estates will much decline, and they sensibly fall in their value already, many Estates being sold, & few Buyers.

This, in a great measure, is owing to the Act of Parliament passed last winter, which lays so many Difficulties upon our Trade, prohibits the Exportation of Lumber, Iron, &c. that it will be scarce possible to make Remittances, which I can, without a Gift of Prophecy, say, will soon be perceived by the London Merchts., & by all the Manufacturers in England.

I have by this Opportunity sent a Box of Magnolia Roots for my Lord Gage, from whom I received great Civilities, and have taken the Freedom to address them to your care.

March 15 1765. To D. Barclay & Sons.

Mr. Penn writes me he never received the Pine Buds, that came by Robertson, whilst I was at Portsmouth, please to enquire of Robertson, if he should be at London when this comes to hand what he did with them, he said when he was here that he delivered them to you, it is but a Trifle, but I am not a little vexed at his Carelessness, as I had promised to supply My Ld Chancellor, and several other great Men by that Canal of Mr. Penn.

May 12th 1765. To Farmer & Galton, Birmingham.

I have your * * * kind present of the Gun, & ye Foils, & Files; every body admires the curious Workmanship of the Gun. * * * We could with the works we now have make 500 Tuns (of Iron) a year, which we might increase as we have proper Situations for erecting more Works, and the Body of Ore is so large as never to be exhausted.

May 19 1765. To D. Barclay & Sons.

I think we have a gloomy Prospect before us, as there are of late some Persons failed, who were no way Suspected, and a probability of some others, as the whisper goes, but what foundation there may be, I cannot say; My Friendship for your worthy House inclines me to hint this much to you, as I know you are connected with a great many people here; The Difficulty of making Remittances, must, of course, distress our Merchants tho' otherwise good & able to discharge their Ingagements. I conceive that our Money, which is yearly decreasing in Quantity, will rather rise in Value, which, as I formerly wrote, together with the Difference of Interest induces me to take my Money out of the Stocks, and invest it in good Security here.

Oct 14 1765. To D. Barclay & Sons.

We are in a very anxious and critical Situation at present about the Stamp Act. As I have wrote to our mutual Friend, Mr Hamilton fully on that head, beg leave to refer you to him for further Information. Our Harvest was very plentiful, not a better being ever known, it is to be hoped our Merchants will be able to make some considerable Remittances to the People they are indebted to at Home, as they are like to Ship Considerably up the Streights, where they are advised Corn will be in demand.

I am now to request a favor of you in behalf of my Cousin Mr. Joseph Shippen, the Secretary of this Province. He remitted a twelvemonth ago * * * £50 Sterling to Mr. Anthony Bacon to procure him thirty-Six Mediterranean Passes, but has never received a Line from him. * * * I beg therefore you would procure for him twenty four Mediterranean passes, and that you would transmit them to him by the first Opportunity. In this Matter, you will not only oblige Mr Shippen and me, but all the Merchants of the Place, who are under the greatest Difficulties for want of them.

[Attached to this letter was the following memorandum of furniture wanted in the handwriting of Anne Allen.]

3 Curtains of a bright crimson Silk & Worsted furniture Damask. The dimension of the Window is as follows. The Height of the Window below the Cornice is ten feet six inches, & the breadth is 4 feet two Inches. The Curtains to be made up in the newest fashion. 2 oval Looking Glasses with papier Mach'e frames. A Wilton Carpet for a room of 27 feet & an half, by twenty five feet. Allowance must be made for the projection of the Chimney. I suppose there are Wilton Carpets of various degrees of goodness, but we should require one of a very moderate price. The size of it must be left to Mr. Barclay. 4 low price fashionable Chandeliers.

December 15 1765. To Samuel Walker & Son, Rotherham.

If your Son continues in the Mind, or has any distant Thoughts of visiting America, I shall readily render him all the Service in my power. Were he here at present we should readily employ him as Manager of our lower Works, called Union, being what I proposed to you & him whilst in England. Mr Hackett removes in April to Andover with his Family, and is to take care of those Works only. We had agreed with one, Mr. Hick, a Friend of Mr Cockshals, that lived some time with Capel Handbury. Esq., from whom he had ample Recommendations, as a person fully qualified to manage a Furnace or Forge, the former of which for these three years past, he had the care of in Maryland. As Mr Hacket was not for some Months to remove, we began with putting the Forge into his Hands, with which, I am sorry to say, he was entirely unacquainted ; And should he want skill with regard to the Furnace, which I believe not to be the case, as he has managed one for the time I mention in Maryland, But as he is, tho' a young man, weakly, and troubled with the Gout & Rheumatism, and from bodily Infirmities not able to go through the active Life that Business requires—I say for these Reasons, I think it will not be well judged to appoint him our Manager, for both, which we intended.

Besides his want of Health, he has a Wife quite unfit for Iron Works, as she appears to be a fine Lady & expects to live with a Delicacy not common in these parts of the World, especially at Iron Works, either in England or here—The Mistress of such a Family as ours ought not to wear Silks, nor spend much of her time in decking her person, or dressing her head, but rather by Care endeavour all she can to promote Oeconomy & Frugality. We shall therefore, tho' with Reluctance, be obliged to part with Mr Hick, when his year is up, as we think him a Sensible Man, and, was he not thus circumstanced, might be useful in Overseeing the Furnace, which indeed is not very mysterious only requiring Assiduity & Care.

Mr Lea, whom you call the young Slitter has now the care of the Slitting Mill, and has brought it into good Order, making every thing much better than our former Slitter. * * * If you could recommend to us a sober skillful man, that will undertake the care of the Forge at Union, we shall willingly allow him Sixty Pounds Sterling a year, and if he behaves well, will increase his wages ten or fifteen pounds more, after we find he is deserving of Incouragement.

December 16, 1765. To D. Barclay & Sons.

I could take up your time in giving you an Account of our Distresses in these parts of the World, but as from your many Correspondents, you must be fully apprised of these matters it appears needless; I take the Freedom however to recommend to you a Pamphlet that States the Dispute between the Mother-Country & us in a masterly manner, & clearly Shows that we are already severely taxed—I think it is the most likely to open the Eyes of the People of England, especially the mercantile part, on whose Knowledge of these matters, & on whose Connections with us, Americans, we have our chief Hopes and Dependance—If we are undone, which will be the Case inevitably if different Measures are not pursued, they must be very great Sufferers. I have sent by Captain Powell One of the Pamphlets to be delivered to you; and many others have from Maryland, (where the

Author is supposed to live) New York, & this place been forwarded to Gentlemen in England.

June 20, 1766. To Robert Davis, Bookseller, Piccadilly.

I should be glad you would continue to send me yearly any curious Books, or Pamphlets that may be published, leaving it to your judgment, not doubting but they will be of such sort as will amuse me, & not be trash, or the common Catch-penny Publications.

October 12th 1767. To Robert Davis, Bookseller, Piccadilly.

I received likewise the two Boxes of Books, but I beg leave to inform you that the person you employed to pack them up, has done it with little care, as the Annual Register instead of being for the last year, was for the year 1764. Many of the Magazines & Reviews were of last year, I mean above a twelvemonth old. I desire in any future parcels you send me that the Magazines & Reviews should not be of those that were publised above three Months before; & should be glad to have them & any curious pamphlets or Books lately printed: but, among the numerous publications there are, you very well know, a great deal of Trash, not worth reading; I shall therefore depend on your Judgment to send for the future such only as will afford me Entertainment.

Nov 8 1767. To D. Barclay & Sons.

The Safe Arrival of our mutual Friend, Mr Hamilton, has given all those with whom he has Connections, and indeed all the respectable part of our Inhabitants great pleasure. We parted with him in great Anxiety, on Account of the Disorder he was troubled with, which, in two Instances, had been fatal to his Family; But the seeing him returned among us in perfect Health, especially as we have had very violent Gales of wind at the time we were hourly expecting him has been an additional Satisfaction.

I have this last week had a Letter from a worthy Friend of mine in New York, who bewails the critical Circumstances of that province. He says there is a general Disposition in the people there to recommend themselves to their Sovereign & their Mother Country, by a dutiful and peaceful Behaviour, and would fain hope that the last Act to provide for the Military people will be satisfactory; tho' the Expence has been great & May be much more so, if an additional Number of Troops be quartered among them; yet they are willing to undergo it in any manner that will not cut up their Liberties by the Roots. And I believe this is the general Sentiment of all America. If we are to be subjected, contrary to our own Consent, to the Impositions & Caprice of every wicked Minister, or General, our Condition will be quite miserable, especially as we have heretofore thought ourselves intitled to the Rights of British Subjects, and were desirous of Showing our Loyalty to our gracious King, by complying, in a legal way, with all the Requisitions made by him: And, in this, a regard to Truth makes me say no province has distinguished itself more than that of New York. During the last War One fifth of their Inhabitants were obliged by ther Acts of Assembly to take the Field with the Regulars, and indeed most of the other Provinces exerted themselves beyond their Abilities. A Sufficient Evidence of this is the large Load of Debt we still labour under. We imagined that this Conduct of ours, would place us, with our Superiors, in a Light of Merit, and So we were told by the Secretaries of State, which we judged was the Canal by which his Majesty's Pleasure was signified to us.

To our great Mortification & Surprize we find that our Trade is unusually Shackled, and Slavery has been intended to be our Lot. A poor Reward, we conceive, for doing what we with so much Cheerfulness have done. If the late Measures are again adopted we shall probably be ruined, but our Mother Country must be also greatly injured, the truth of which time will, if this dreaded Event happen, make manifest.

Our Assembly are very Sensible of the kind patronage and friendship shown us by the Committee of Merchants, and have ordered their Agents to return them their warmest Thanks. Some Expressions in the Committee's Letter to our Merchants recommending Submission in points that they construed would be destructive of their Libertys, and the fear of disobliging them by any Reasonings on these heads, prevented them from answering their Letters, and expressing their Gratitude for their benevolent & kind Assistance afforded them in their then distress. But I then thought, & now think, that they did not Judge that matter well, as it must appear in the Light of Ingratitude, when the Reasons of their not doing it would not be known. I beg pardon for Saying so much on a Subject that has been so much canvassed of late.

Our late Manager * * * had * * * mismanaged our Concerns; which together with the making

Iron an enumerated Commodity, has made us not pleased that we have imbarked so deeply in that way.

May 1st 1768. To Colin Drummond, Quebec.

I had the Honor to be known to your worthy Brother, formerly in this part of the World, and had the pleasure of his Acquaintance about 4 years Since in London, we being next door Neighbours in Golden Square.

October 29 1768. To David & John Barclay.

Give me leave to acknowledge your Sundry Favors, to which I should have wrote Answers; But, as I had nothing material to trouble you with, I have been silent for some time: But, as at present there seems to be a black Cloud hanging over America, I crave your patience in hearing my Sentiments of the present posture of Affairs, and, give me leave to say, I am allowed to be one of the most moderate of my Country men.

The gross Misrepresentations of Governor Bernard (who, was his true Character as well known with you as it is in America, would be little regarded) have very undeservedly inflamed the Nation. I think, if the Indiscretion of the Mob be treasonable & rebellious, our fellow Subjects in Britain may more justly be chargeable with these Crimes than any Americans; and they are more excusable, when designing men, in order to curry favor with the Ministry, are working up the Dregs of the people to these follys; which has certainly been the Case. The American Assemblies have done no Act, but that of petitioning for Redress of Grievances, in which they are unanimous in all the Colonies; And as you may be assured, that it is the determined Resolution of all

America not to take up Arms against their Mother Country, and the only War they will wage with her, is to curtail their Superfluities, & supply themselves with Necessaries, which the unconstitutional Taxes & Duties, as they conceive them to be, disable them from importing from England; and, upon the whole, to have as little Intercourse as possible, in the Trading Ways, with their unkind Mother, who, at present, they say, treats them as Slaves, and not as Children. We have in this Province, been willing to wait with patience till the Nation was better informed, & doubted not the Interest of the Mother Country, so closely connected with ours, would at length cause our Hardships to be taken off. But we stand amazed at the sending over Men of War & Soldiers at a great expense to the Nation to fight Windmills. Whenever they come, or in what Numbers, they will find the Americans as peaceable, I might say, much more so than the people of England, & might add, much more virtuous, consequently very tenacious of their Liberties, but that only in a Constitutional Way. We are assured that things, if we continue in a State of Moderation, will shortly be seen in their true light, and every thing be put upon a just footing; And that in the End we shall be allowed to give our own Money, without which the Wounds, now open, will not heal for an Age to come.

The Distress on every body's mind, and on Mine among others, makes me take the freedom to say thus much, which I trust to your Goodness to excuse. * * * Upon examining my Books, I found I had over run the Constable. The fitting out my Children in the Matrimonial way has been an expensive Job to me, tho' attended with a high pleasure to see them well settled.
* * * Our Mutual Friend, Mr. Coleman, is arrived

in as good health as could be expected, and thinks himself quite relieved from his Cancerous Complaint.

My Daughter, Margaret, desires her Compliments to Mrs. John Barclay, and begs she would choose her a fashionable Silk for a Negligee, about the price of that sent to Miss Oswald. * * * I have placed your Ancestor's Book in my Library, and return my hearty Thanks to your worthy Father for the present of so valuable an Edition of that excellent Performance.

November 7. 1769. To David & John Barclay.

My long Silence has not, in any manner, proceeded from a want of an unfeigned Friendship, & a grateful Sense of your many Kindnesses to me & my Family, which have, and always will make a lasting Impression on my Mind; But that nothing occurred worthy of your Notice.

I now beg leave to condole with you for the Loss of your worthy Father. Instances of so great Merit, & truly Christian Virtues are much too rare in this world. He died full of years, and those spent faithfully; and, no doubt, receives the Reward of his Doings. I knew him forty-six years, great part of which I had dealings with him, during which time I always highly esteemed him, & shall ever revere his Memory.

I know that you do not choose to have any Detail of our internal Politics, for which reason have not, especially since my return from England, given you any trouble that way; I may, however, go so far as to tell you, all our Contentions, which, you very well know, are incident to free Countries, are quite subsided, at least for a time.

The wrong-headed Schemes of your Side of the Water have fully taken up our Attention, for so I may call them, as they are very injurious to Britain, & ruinous to us. Since I left England, the many Restrictions on Trade have greatly affected us. Our Debtors prove often insolvent; and if we sell the Estates of such as have any, there appear to be few or no Buyers; and, if they are sold, it is often at a third of what used to be thought the value. Indeed I can assure you that property is lowered near half its value in most of, if not all North America; particularly Iron Works, in which Concern many people, by the Incouragement from England, in taking off the Duties, had of late imbarked, have their Works in a manner knocked up. The enumerating of that Commodity has put most of our Works to a stand, and Mr Turner & I intend to let ours, which is one of the most considerable in America, lie still till better times.

I had a good deal of Conversation with Col. Scott, a Member of Parliament, who last year travelled through the Colonies, who agreed with me that most of the late Commercial Regulations were absurd, & injurious to both Countries; and he with great Confidence assured me that they would be repealed, and Matters put upon the old System. The Ministry write our Governors that the Duty on Paint & Glass will be repealed: But such a palliative will do little good, as they are Commodities which we can either procure among ourselves, or do without. The Whole, late Commercial Regulations must be done away, & things put in their former Channel, or our Grievances will be redressed only in name. However, many judicious people among us are Sanguine in their hopes that their present Oppressions & Distresses will, in the end, be useful to us, & will teach us the necessity of more Industry & Frugality. They say the good Work is already begun ; and that if things remain in their present State for a very few years, good will rise out of evil; That it is likely to be excellent Physic to the Body Politic. Our people have left off going to the Stores to buy what they usually took up, which they now make in their own Families. The Storekeepers universally complain that they do not vend one half of the Goods they used to do. Even the lawyers alledge their business is in a manner at an end, as there are very few Contracts, of course few Lawsuits.

Upon the whole I believe it would be for the Interest of these Colonies that these things should be continued on us for some time. Tho' for want of Trade, we could not grow rich ; yet, I believe we should be soon out of Debt to Britain, as well as to our Merchants ; And, I think, more cautious for the future in plunging in to the Luxury too common among us within these fifteen years past.

Jany 4 1770. To Rob. Davis.

I some time since, received a small Package of Books, Pamphlets, Magazines, &c. which I presume came from you. * * * I have perused the several Tracts of Husbandry, & some Letters from Mr Baldwin, which gave me pleasure ; he describes some Instruments, or Ploughs, in the Drillway and directs where they may be had. I beg you would procure for me his Drill, Horse-hoe, & Horse-ploughs and send them to the care of Messrs Barclay to be forwarded to me, with some directions how to use them if that should be necessary. * * * I must depend on your goodness to excuse me for giving you this trouble, which I hope you will be so kind as to do, as I am sure it would give you pleasure to have the useful hints in your Re Rustica put into practice, even in this part of the World. Very few persons in this Country have made more experiments in the farming way than I have, and, in this latter Stage of Life, my Books, & my little Farm are great part of my Amusement.

Jany 4th 1770. To David & John Barclay.

My Daughter Margaret wants a couple of dozen of white Silk Stockings; please, therefore, to send them by one of the first Spring Ships, and let them be Strong, and somewhat larger than the middle Size. I presume ere that time the Revenue Acts will be repealed, or I can prevail on the Committee of Merchants to have them delivered to her, or, at least part of them.

APPENDIX.

A PROTEST

Presented to the

HOUSE OF ASSEMBLY,

By the Subscribers, at the Close of the late Debate there, concerning the sending

MR. FRANKLIN

As an Assistant to our AGENT, at the Court of Great-Britain.

We whose Names are hereunto subscribed, do object and *protest* against the Appointment of the Person proposed as an Agent of this Province, for the following reasons.

First. Because we believe him to be the Chief Author of the Measures pursued by the late Assembly, which have occasioned such Uneasiness and Destraction among the good People of this Province.

Secondly. Because we believe his fixed enmity to the Proprietors will preclude all Accommodations of our Disputes with them, even on just and reasonable Terms; —So that for these two Reasons, we are filled with the most affecting Apprehensions, that the Petitions lately transmitted to England, will be made use of to produce a Change of Government, contrary to the Intention of the Petitioners; the greatest part of whom, we are persuaded, only designed thereby to obtain a Compliance with some equitable Demand.—And thus, by such an Appointment, we, and a vast Number of our most worthy Constituents, are deprived of all hopes of ever seeing an End put to the fatal Dissentions of our Country; it being our firm Opinion, that any further Prosecution of the Measures for a Change of Government at this Time, will lay the Foundations of Unceasing Feuds, and all the Miseries of Confusion, among the People we represent, and their Posterity.—This step gives us the more lively Affliction, as it is taken at the very Moment, when we are informed by a Member of this House, that the Governor has assured Him of his having received Instructions from the Proprietors, on their hearing of our late Dispute, to give his Assent to the Taxation of their Estates in the same manner that the Estates of other Persons are to be taxed, and also to confirm, for the Public use, the several *Squares,* formerly claimed by the City ; On which Subjects, we make no doubt, the Governor would have sent a Message to the House, if this had been the usual Time of doing Business, and he had not been necessarily absent to meet the Assembly of the lower Counties.— And therefore we cannot but anxiously regret that, at a Time when the Proprietors have shown such a Disposition, this House should not endeavor to cultivate the same, and obtain from them every reasonable Demand that can be made on the part of the People ; in vigorously insisting on which, we would most earnestly unite with the rest of the House.

Thirdly. Because the Gentleman proposed, we are informed, is very unfavorably thought of by several of his Majesty's Ministers ; and we are humbly of Opinion, that it will be disrespectful to our most Gracious Sovereign, and disadvantageous to ourselves and our constituents, to employ such a Person as Agent.

Fourthly. Because the Proposal of the Person mentioned, is so extremely disagreeable to a very great Number of the most serious and reputable Inhabitants of this Province of all Denominations and Societies (one Proof of which is, his having been rejected, both by this City and County at the last Election, though he had represented the former in Assembly for 14 Year) that we are convinced no Measure this House can adopt, will tend so much to inflame the Resentments and imbitter the Divisions of the good People of this Province, as his appointment to be our Agent—And we cannot but sincerely lament, that the Peace and Happiness of Pennsylvania should be sacrificed for the Promotion of a Man, who cannot be advanced but by the Convulsions of his Country.

Fifthly. Because the unnecessary haste with which this House has acted in proceeding to this Appointment (without making a small Adjournment, tho' requested by many Members, to consult our Constituents on the Matters to be decided, and) even before their Speaker has been presented to the King's Representative, tho' we are informed that the Governor will be in Town the Beginning of next Week;—may subject us to the Censures and very heavy Displeasure of our most gracious Sovereign and his Ministers.

Sixthly. Because the Gentleman propos'd has heretofore ventured, contrary to an Act of Assembly, to place the * public Money in the Stocks, whereby this Province suffered a loss of £.6000; and that Sum, added to £.5000 granted for his Expense, makes the whole Cost of his former Voyage to England, amount to ELEVEN THOUSAND POUNDS; which expensive kind of Agency we do not chuse to imitate, and burden the Public with unnecessary loads of Debt. For these and other Reasons we should think ourselves guilty of betraying the Rights of Pennsylvania, if we should presumptuously commit them to the Discretion of a Man, against whom so many and just Objections present themselves.

Lastly. We being extremely desirous to avert the Mischiefs apprehended from the intended Appointment, and as much as in us lies to promote Peace and Unan-

---
*The Money here meant was a Sum granted by Parliament as an Indemnification for part of our Expences in the late War, which by Act of Assembly was ordered for its better security to be placed in the Bank.

imity among us and our Constituents, do humbly propose to the House, that if they will agree regularly to appoint any ⸹ Gentleman of Integrity, Abilities, and Knowledge in England, to assist Mr. Jackson as our Agent, under a Restriction not to present the Petitions for a Change of our Government, or any of them, to the King or his Ministers, unless an express Order for that Purpose be hereafter given by the Assembly of this Province; we will not give it any Opposition: But if such an Appointment should be made, we must insist (as we cannot think it a necessary one) that our Constituents, already labouring under heavy Debts, be not burthened with fresh Impositions on that Account; and therefore, in Condescension to the Members, who think another Agent necessary, we will concur with them, if they approve of this Proposal, in paying such Agent at our own Expence.

October 26, 1764.

JOHN DICKINSON,
DAVID Mc.CANAUGHY,
JOHN MONTGOMERY,
ISAAC SAUNDERS,
GEORGE TAYLOR,
WILLIAM ALLEN,
THOMAS WILLING,
GEORGE BRYAN,
AMOS STRETTELL,
HENRY KEPPELE.

⸹Dr. Fothergill was mentioned by the Subscribers as a proper Person.

REMARKS
ON A LATE
PROTEST

Against the Appointment of Mr. Franklin an Agent for this *Province.*

I have generally passed over, with a silent Disregard, the nameless abusive Pieces that have been written against me; and tho' this Paper, called a Protest, is signed by some respectable Names, I was, nevertheless, inclined to treat it with the same Indifference; but as the Assembly is therein reflected on upon my Account, it is thought more my Duty to make some Remarks upon it.

I would first observe then, that this Mode of *Protesting* by the Minority, with a string of Reasons against the Proceedings of the Majority of the House of Assembly, is quite new among us; the present is the second we have had of the kind, and both within a few Months. It is unknown to the Practice of the House of Commons, or of any House of Representatives in *America*, that I have heard of; and seems an affected Imitation of the Lords in Parliament, which can by no Means become Assembly-men of *America.* Hence appears the Absurdity of the Complaint, that the House refused the Protest an

Entry on their Minutes. The Protestors know that they are not, by any Custom or Usage, intitled to such an Entry, and that the Practice here is not only useless in itself, but would be highly inconvenient to the House, since it would probably be thought necessary for the Majority also to enter their Reasons, to justify themselves to their Constituents, whereby the Minutes would be incumbered, and the Public Business obstructed. More especially will it be found inconvenient, if such Protests are made use of as a new form of Libelling, as the Vehicles of personal Malice, and as Means of giving to private Abuse the Appearance of a Sanction, as public Acts. Your Protest, Gentlemen, was therefore properly refused; and since it is no Part of the Proceedings of Assembly, one may with more Freedom examine it.

Your first Reason against my Appointment is, that you "believe me to be the chief Author of the Measures "pursued by the last Assembly, which have occasioned "such Uneasiness and Distraction among the good People "of this Province. I shall not dispute my Share in those Measures; I hope they are such as will in time do Honour to all that were concerned in them. But you seem mistaken in the Order of Time: It was the Uneasiness and Distraction among the good People of the Province that occasioned the Measures; the Province was in Confusion before they were taken, and they were pursued in order to prevent such Uneasiness and Distraction for the future. Make one step farther back, and you will find Proprietary Injustice supported by Proprietary Minions and Creatures, the original Cause of all our Uneasiness and Distractions.

Another of your Reasons is, "that I am, as you are "informed, very unfavourably thought of by several of "his Majesty's Ministers." I apprehend, Gentlemen, that your Informer is mistaken. He indeed has taken great Pains to give unfavourable Impressions of me, and perhaps may flatter himself, that it is impossible so much true Industry should be totally without Effect. His long Success in maiming or murdering all the Reputations that stand in his Way, which has been the dear Delight and constant Employment of his Life, may likewise have given him some just Ground for Confidence that he has, as they call it, *done for me*, among the rest. But, as I said before, I believe he is mistaken. For what have I done that they should think unfavourably of me? It cannot be my constantly and uniformly promoting the Measures of the Crown, ever since I had any Influence in the Province. It cannot, surely, be my promoting the Change from a Proprietary to a Royal Government. If indeed I had, by Speeches and Writings endeavoured to make his Majesty's Government universally odious in the Province. If I had harangued by the Week, to all Comers and Goers, on the pretended Injustice and Oppressions of Royal Government, and the Slavery of the People under it. If I had written traiterous Papers to this Purpose, and got them translated into other Languages, to give his Majesty's foreign Subjects here those horrible Ideas of it. If I had declared, written and printed, that "the King's little Finger we should find heavier than the Proprietors whole Loins," with regard to our Liberties: *then indeed* might the Ministers be supposed to think unfavorably of me. But these are no Exploits for a Man who holds a profitable Office under the Crown, and can expect to hold it no longer than he behaves with the Fidelity and Duty that becomes every good Subject. They are only for Officers of Proprietary Appointment, who hold their Commissions during his, and not the King's Pleasure; and who, by dividing among themselves, and their Relations, Offices of many Thousands a Year, enjoyed by Proprietary Favour, *feel* where to place their Loyalty. I wish they were as good Subjects to his Majesty;—and perhaps they may be so, when the Proprietary interferes no longer.

Another of your Reasons is, "that the Proposal of me "for an Agent is extremely disagreeable to a very great "Number of the most serious and reputable Inhabitants "of the Province; and the Proof is, my having been "rejected at the last Election, tho' I had represented the "City in Assembly for 14 Years."

And do those of you, Gentlemen, reproach me with this, who among near Four Thousand Votes, had scarcely a Score more than I had? It seems then, that your *Elections* were very near being *Rejections*, and thereby furnishing the same Proof in your Case that you produce in mine, of your being likewise extremely disagreeable to a very great Number of the most serious and reputable People. Do you honourable Sir, reproach me with this, who for almost twice 14 Years have been rejected (if *not being chosen* is *to be rejected*) by the same People, and unable with all your Wealth and Connections, and the Influence they give you, to obtain an Election in the County where you reside, and the City where you were born, and are best known, have been obliged to accept a seat from one of the out Counties, the remotest of the Province!—It is known, Sir, to the Persons who proposed me, that I was first chosen against my own Inclination, and against my Entreaties that I might be suffered to remain a private Man. In none of the 14 Elections you mention did I ever appear as a Candidate. I never did, directly or indirectly solicit any Man's Vote. For six of the Years in which I was annually chosen, I was absent, residing in England; during all which Time, your secret and open Attacks upon my Character and Reputation were incessant; and yet you gained no Ground. And can you really, Gentlemen, find Matter of Triumph in this *Rejection* as you call it? A Moments Reflection on the Means by which it was obtained, must make you ashamed of it.

Not only my duty to the Crown, in carrying the Post-Office Act more duly into Execution, was made use of to exasperate the Ignorant, as if I was encreasing my own Profits, by picking their Pockets; but my very Zeal in opposing the Murderers, and supporting the Authority of Government, and even my Humanity, with regard to the innocent *Indians* under our Protection, were mustered among my Offences, to stir up against me those religious Bigots, who are of all Savages the most brutish. Add to this the numberless Falsehoods propogated as Truths, and the many Perjuries procured among the wretched Rabble brought to swear themselves intitled to a Vote; —and yet so *poor a Superiority* obtained at all this Expence of Honour and Conscience! Can this, Gentlemen, be Matter of Triumph! Enjoy it then. Your Exultation, however, was short.—Your Artifices did not prevail everywhere; nor your double Tickets, and whole Boxes of forged Votes. A great Majority of the new chosen Assembly were of the old Members, and remain uncorrupted. They still stand firm for the People, and will obtain Justice from the Proprietaries. But what does that avail to you who are in the Proprietary Interest? And what Comfort can it afford you, when by the Assembly's choice of an Agent, it appears that the same, to you obnoxious, Man, (notwithstanding all your venomous Invectives against him) still retains so great a Share of the public Confidence?

But "this Step, you say, gives you the more lively

"Affliction, as it is taken at the *very Moment* when you "were informed by a Member of the House, that the "Governor had assured him of his having received In- "structions from the Proprietaries, to give his Assent to "the Taxation of their Estates, in the *same Manner* that "the Estates of other Persons are to be taxed; and also "*to confirm*, for the public Use, the several Squares form- "erly *claimed* by the City." O the Force of Friendship! the Power of Interest! What Politeness they infuse into a Writer, and what *delicate* Expressions they pro- duce! The Dispute between the Proprietaries and us was about the *Quantum*, the *Rate* of their Taxation, and not about the *Manner;* but now, when all the World, condemns them for requiring a partial Exemption of their Estates, and they are forced to submit to an honest Equality, 'tis called "*assenting* to be taxed in the *same* "*Manner* with the People:"—Their *Restitution* of five public Squares in the Plan of the City, which they had near forty Years unjustly and dishonourably seized and detained from us, directing their Surveyor to map Streets over them (in order to turn them into Lots) and their Officers to sell a Part of them; this their **Disgorging** is softly called *confirming* them for the public Use; and instead of the plain Words *formerly given* to the City, by the first Proprietary their Father, we have the cautious pretty Expression of "formerly *claimed* by the City." Yes, not only *formerly* but *always* claimed, ever since they were *promised* and *given* to encourage the Settlers, and ever will be *claimed* till we are put in actual Pos- session of them. 'Tis pleasant, however to see how lightly and tenderly you trip over these Matters, as if you trod upon Eggs.—But that "VERY MOMENT," that precious Moment! why was it so long delayed? Why were those healing Instructions so long withheld and concealed from the People? They were, it seems, brought over by Mr. *Allen.* Intelligence was received by various Hands from *London,* that Orders were sent by the Proprietaries, from which great Hopes were entertained of an Accommodation. Why was the Bringing and Delivery of such Orders so long *denied?* The Reason is easily understood. Messieurs *Barclays,* Friends to both Proprietaries and People, wished for that Gentleman's happy Arrival, hoping his *Influence,* added to the *Power* and *Commissions* the Proprietaries had vested him with, might prove effectual in restoring Harmony and Tranquility among us;—but he, it seems, hoped his *Influence* might do the Business, without those Additions.—There appeared on his Arrival from Prospect, from sundry Circumstances, of a Change to be made in the House by the approaching Election. The Proprietary Friends and Creatures knew the Heart of their Master, and how extremely disagreeable to him that *equal Taxation,* the *Restitution,* and the other *Concessions* to be made for the Sake of a Reconciliation, must necessarily be. They hoped therefore to spare him all those Mortifications, and thereby secure a greater Portion of his Favour. Hence the Instructions were not produced to the last Assembly, though they arrived before the *September* Sitting, when the Governor was in Town, and actually did Business with the House. Nor to the new Assembly were they mentioned, till the *"very Moment"* the fatal Moment, when the House were on the Point of chusing that wicked Adversary of the Proprietary to be an Agent for the Province in *England.*

But I have, you say, a "fixed Enmity to the proprie-"taries," and you believe it will preclude all Accommo-"dation of our disputes with them, even on just and "reasonable Terms."—And why do you think I have a fixed Enmity to the Proprietaries?—I have never had any personal difference with them. I am no Land-Jobber, and therefore have never had any Thing to do with their Land-Office or officers;—if I had, probably, like others, I might have been obliged to truckle to their Measures, or have had like Causes of Complaint. But our private Interests never clashed, and all their Resentment against me, and mine to them, has been on the public Account. Let them do Justice to the People of *Pennsylvania*, act honourably by the Citizens of *Philadelphia*, and become honest Men; my Enmity, if that's of any Consequence, ceases from the "*very Moment;*" and, as soon as I possibly can, I promise to love, honour and respect them.—In the mean Time, why do you "believe "it will preclude all Accommodation with them on just "and reasonable Terms?" Do you not boast that their gracious Condescensions are in the Hands of the Governor, and that, "if this had been the usual Time for "Business, his Honour would have sent them down in a "Message to the House." How then can my going to *England* prevent this Accommodation? The Governor can call the House when he pleases, and, one would think, that, at least in your Opinion my being out of the Way, would be a favourable Circumstance. For then, by, "cultivating the Disposition shown by the Proprie-"taries, every *reasonable Demand* that can be made on "the Part of the People might be obtained; in vigorously "insisting on which, you promise to unite most earnestly "with the rest of the House."—It seems then we have "*reasonable Demands*" to make, and as you call them a little higher, *equitable Demands*. This is much for Proprietary Minions to own;—but you are all growing better, in Imitation of your Master, which is indeed very commendable. And if the Accommodation there should fail, I hope that though you dislike the person a Majority of two to one in the House having thought fit to appoint an Agent, you will nevertheless, in Duty to your Country, continue the noble Resolution of uniting with the rest of the House, in vigorously insisting on that *Equity* and *Justice*, which such an Union will undoubtedly obtain for us.

I pass over the trivial Charge against the Assembly, that they, "acted with *unnecessary Haste* in proceeding "to this Appointment, without making a small Adjourn- "ment," &c. and your affected Apprehensions of Danger from that Haste. The Necessity of Expedition on this Occasion is as obvious to every one out of Doors as it was to those within; and the Fears you mention are not, I fancy, considerable enough to break your Rest.—I come then to your high Charge against me, "That I heretofore "ventured, *contrary* to an Act of Assembly, to place the "Public Money in the Stocks, whereby this Province "suffered a Loss of 6000£ and that Sum added to the "5000£ granted for my Expences, makes the whole Cost "of my former Voyage to *England* amount to ELEVEN "THOUSAND POUNDS!"—How wisely was that Form in our Laws contrived, which when a Man is arraigned for his Life, requires the Evidence to speak *the Truth*, the *whole Truth*, and *nothing but the Truth!* The Reason is manifest. A Falsehood may destroy the Innocent; so may *Part of the Truth* without *the Whole;* and a Mixture of Truth and Falsehood may be full as pernicious. You, Mr. Chief Justice, and the other Justices among the Protestors, and you, Sir, who are a Counsellor at Law, must all of you be well acquainted with this excellent Form; and when you arraign'd my Reputation (dearer to me than Life) before the Assembly, and now at the respectable Tribunal of the Public, would it not have well become your Honours to have had some small Regard at least to the Spirit of that Form; You might have mentioned, that the Direction of the Act to lodge the Money in the Bank, subject to the Drafts of the Trustees of the Loan Office here, was impracticable; that the Bank refused to receive it on those Terms, it being contrary to their settled Rules to take Charge of Money subject to the Orders of unknown People, living in distant Countries.—You might have mentioned, that the House being informed of this, and having no immediate Call for the Money, did themselves adopt the Measure of placing it in the Stocks, which then were low; where it might on a Peace produce a considerable profit, and in the mean time accumulate an Interest: That they even passed a Bill, directing the subsequent Sums granted by the Parliament, to be placed with the former; That the Measure was prudent and safe: and that the Loss arose, not from *placing* the Money IN the Stocks, but from the imprudent and unnecessary DRAWING IT OUT at the very time when they were lowest, on some slight uncertain Rumours of a Peace concluded: That if the Assembly had let it remain another Year, instead of loosing they would have gained *Six Thousand Pounds;* and that after all, since the Exchange, at which they sold their Bills, was near *Twenty per Cent.* higher when they drew, than when the Stocks were purchased, the Loss was far from being so great as you represent it. All these Things you might have said, for they are, and you know them to be, Part of the *whole Truth;*—but they would have spoiled your Accusation. The late Speaker of your honourable House, Mr. *Norris*, who has, I suppose, all my letters to him, and Copies of his own to me, relating to that Transaction, can testify with how much Integrity and Clearness I managed the whole Affair.—All the

House were sensible of it, being from time to time fully
acquainted with the Facts. If I had gone to Gaming in
the Stocks with the Public Money, and through my
fault a Sum was lost, as your Protest would Insinuate,
why was I not censured and punished for it when I
returned? You, honourable Sir (my Enemy of seven
Years standing) was then in the House. You were
appointed on the Committee for examining my Accounts;
you reported that you found them just, and signed that
Report*. I never solicited the employ of Agent: I
made no Bargain for my future Service, when I was
ordered to England by the Assembly; nor did they vote
me any Salary. I lived there near six Years at my own
expence and I made no Charge or Demand when I came
home. You, Sir, of all others, was the very Member
that proposed (for the Honor and Justice of the House)
a Compensation to be made me of the *Five Thousand
Pounds* you mention. Was it with an intent to reproach
me thus publicly for accepting it? I thanked the House

---

*Report of the Committee on *Benjamin Franklin's* Accounts.

In Obedience to the Order of the House, we have examined the Accounts of Benjamin
Franklin, *Esq, with the Vouchers to us produced in Support thereof, and do find the same
Account to be just, and that he has expended in the immediate Service of this Province, the
Sum of* Seven Hundred and Fourteen Pounds, Ten Shillings *and* Seven-pence, *out of the
Sum of* Fifteen Hundred Pounds *Sterling, to him remitted and paid, exclusive of any Allowance or Charge for his Support and Service for the Province.*

February 19, 1763.	JOHN MORTON,	JOSEPH FOX,
	WILLIAM ALLEN,	JOHN HUGHES,
	JOHN ROSS,	SAMUEL RHOADS,
	JOHN MOOR,	JOHN WILKINSON,
		ISAAC PEARSON.

*The House taking the foregoing Report of the Committee of Accounts into Consideration,
and having spent some time therein,*

Resolved,

That the Sum of Five Hundred Pounds *Ster. per Annum be allowed and given to* Benjamin Franklin, *Esq: late Agent for the Province of* Pennsylvania *at the Court of Great-Britain, during his Absence of six Years from his Business and Connections, in the Service of the Public; and that the Thanks of this House be also given to the said Gentleman by Mr. Speaker, from the Chair, as well for the faithful discharge of his Duty to this Province in particular, as for the many and important Services done* America *in general, during his Residence in* Great-Britain.

Thursday, March 31, 1763.

Pursuant to a Resolve of the Nineteenth of last Month, that the Thanks of this House be given to Benjamin Franklin, *Esq; for his many Services not only to the Province of* Pennsylvania, *but to* America *in general, during his late Agency at the Court of* Great-Britain, *the same were this Day accordingly given in Form from the Chair.—To which Mr.* Franklin, *respectfully addressing himself to the Speaker, made Answer, That he was thankful to the House, for the very handsome and generous Allowance they had been pleased to make him for his Services; but that the Approbation of this House was, in his Estimation, far above every other kind of Recompence."*

Votes, 1763.

for it then, and I thank you now for proposing it: Tho' you, who have lived in *England*, can easily conceive, that besides the Prejudice to my private Affairs by my Absence, a *Thousand Pounds* more would not have reimbursed me. The Money voted was immediately paid me. But, if I had occasioned the loss of *Six Thousand Pounds* to the Province, here was a fair opportunity of securing easily the greatest Part of it; why was not the *Five Thousand Pounds* deducted, and the Remainder called for?—The Reason is, This Accusation was not then invented.—Permit me to add, that supposing the whole *Eleven Thousand Pounds* an expence occasioned by my Voyage to *England*, yet the Taxation of the Proprietary estate now established, will, when valued by Years Purchase, be found in time an Advantage to the Public, far exceeding that Expence. And if the Expence is at present a Burthen, the Odium ought to lie on those who, by their Injustice, made the Voyage necessary, and not on me, who only submitted to the Orders of the House, in undertaking it.

I am now to take Leave (perhaps a last Leave) of the Country I love, and in which I have spent the greatest Part of my Life.—Esto Perpetua.—I wish every kind of Prosperity to my Friends,—and I forgive my Enemies.

Philadelphia, Nov. 5, 1764.   B. FRANKLIN.

AN ANSWER TO
MR. FRANKLIN'S REMARKS
ON A LATE PROTEST.

A day or two after Mr. Franklin's departure for England, having seen his remarks in the hands of a gentleman, I gave them a cursory perusal; but found them so replete with bitter calumnies and gross evasions, that I judged them unworthy of any further notice.

But being since told that his deluded partizans have begun to consider this neglect of his performance, as an argument of its unanswerable nature; I shall bestow a few hours (since no abler hand has thought it worth while) in order to convince them, if possible, that the real design of this their redoubted champion was not to elucidate, but to disguise and conceal the truth; which, it must be allowed, according to his usual custom, he has very artfully, but not honestly done.

He sets out with telling us, that he has *generally* passed over with a silent disregard, the nameless pieces that have been written against him. The publick knows what sort of disregard he has shown to the pieces written against him, and to their supposed authors. At present I pass on to the more material parts of his performance, which for my own sake I could have wished a little more methodical, and that the *calumny-part* had not been so indiscriminately blended with what he would have to pass as the *argumentative part.* I must, however, try to separate them as well as I can, for the greater clearness in writing; and shall begin with his remarks on the *Protest,* before I proceed to his shameful abuse of the *Protestors.*

His first remark is that—"the mode of *protesting* by "the minority, against the proceedings of the majority "of the house of assembly, is quite *new* among us;—is "unknown to the practice of the house of commons, or "of any house of representatives in America, and seems "an affected imitation of the lords in parliament, &c."

It is acknowledged that *protesting* may not be an usual method in American assemblies, nor of late years practiced in the house of commons in England, which is a very numerous body. But, in a constitution like ours, where there is no legislative council, it may not always be improper; and if the Remarker has nothing to urge against the *reason* or *necessity* of a thing, but its novelty, it will have but little weight. When cases and emergencies arise which are new and unprecedented in their nature, a new and unprecedented mode of proceeding against them, may become indispensably necessary.

If, for instance, contrary to the uses of the Commons in England, whose votes and transactions are regularly laid before their constituents from day to day, a house of assembly in America should keep their proceedings private for a whole year, and are, during that time, pursuing measures which are conceived fundamentally subversive of the constitution; and if those Members, who conscientiously oppose these measures, cannot even have so much as their *yeas* and *nays* made known to their constituents, to rescue them from odium which they have not merited—I say if such a case as this could possibly happen, then surely it becomes both a publick and private duty in those who are against such measures, not only to oppose them by every means in their power (by reasons both spoken and written) but likewise immediately, openly, and avowedly, to lay the whole before their constituents, from whom they derive their power, and to whom they are accountable for their conduct.

Had it not been for a publication of this kind made by three Members, (it matters not whether it was called a *Protest* or reasons of dissent offered in writing) I say, had it not been for a seasonable publication of this kind some time ago, and the papers that soon afterwards followed it, the late Assembly might have made their measures for a change of government pass silently home to England as the sense of the People, without their constituents having any opportunity, upon their own certain knowledge of these measures, to represent dutifully to our most gracious sovereign, that they were unauthorized by the people, contrary to our Charter, and therefore, by the very tenor of it, "void and of no effect." Such a silence as this would, no doubt, have very well suited the ambitious and destructive schemes of the Remarker, and would have saved him from some share, perhaps, of the general odium which he has the mortification to bear from the good people of this province, for his most wicked attempt to deprive them of their present excellent constitution, in the very face of their charter, and without their consent or authority.

It is no wonder then that this *mode of protesting* should not be agreeable to him, and that he should pour forth such abundance of abuse against all who think proper to follow that mode; tho', in fact, the *Protest* he has remarked on, was never offered by more than one of the signers to be entered on the Minutes, but was only read as the sum of the reasons that had been offered in the debate, and which, the House were told, would be laid before the publick. As the speaker of the House had not been presented to the governor, nor taken the usual qualifications to his majesty's person and government, most of the Members who signed the paper, printed in the nature of a *Protest*, did not think it necessary to press it on the House, which they judged, under these circumstances, could not regularly proceed to any business.

But the Remarker objects against this *mode* for another reason. He says "The Minutes would thereby be incumbered, &c." This may be of some weight with those who *pay* for the Minutes; but surely, you Mr. PRINTER* who *print* these Minutes and are *paid* for them, cou'd not make this a serious objection. It is a pity, you had not learn'd this saving wisdom some years ago, when you *encumbered* the Minutes with such loads of scurrilous messages of your own drawing, and such long reports put together from law books, old histories and journals, that for *printing, copying*, and other services, you and your son shared between you near *two thousand pounds* of the publick money. But you had not then got yourself saddled upon this province, with a large annual salary as our ambassador extraordinary to England.

I shall now drop you, Sir, as Mr. Printer, and follow you in your higher characters of Mr. Ambassador, Mr. Post-master, (or by whatever other name you would be pleased to be called) while you go on modestly arguing your own cause, and proclaiming your own merits against the *Protestors*.

The first reason offered against you by these respect-

---

* The calling gentlemen by their professions and offices I find to be a favorite method of the Remarker, and I hope he will not be angry with me for adopting it as occasion offers. See page 95—"You, Mr. Chief Justice and other Justices among the Protesters, and you, Sir, who are a Counsellor at Law."

able gentlemen, is a very strong and clear one. They "believe you to be the chief author of the measures pur"sued by the late Assembly, which have occasioned such "uneasiness and distraction among the good people of "this province"—With what a poor quibble do you pretend to answer this most grievous charge? Can any person but yourself, doubt what *measures* the Protestors mean? Do they not expressly specify them to be those identical "measures which occasioned such distractions among the people"—"measures likewise pursued by the late assembly"—Now, is it not universally known that there was no uneasiness or distraction among the people on account of any measures pursued by the late Assembly, but their attempt to change the constitution of this province, of their own mere authority, and contrary to the very tenor of our charter.

The *Protestors* believed that you was—"the chief "author of these measures" and you yourself do "not dispute your share in them." The argument of the Protestors, then, against giving you any discretionary powers over the liberties of the people, which they had reason to think you would make a willing sacrifice of to your own ambition, was a strong and conclusive one. And do you think to answer it by a ridiculous play upon words—"saying that the distraction and uneasiness of "the people were not occasioned by the measuses, but the "measures by the distraction, &c?" Such a subterfuge as this will not answer the charge brought against you by the Protestors. No, it will stick to you, and continue your name as odious to the next generation, perhaps, as it is to this.

You object to another reason of the Protestors against you, *viz.*—"that you are, as they are informed, very "unfavourably thought of by several of his majesty's "ministers"—You puzzle yourself to account for this dislike of some of the king's ministers to you, abuse your accusers, and proclaim your own services to the crown, which will yield you but little cause of boasting when they are fairly stated to you. But be that as it will, the fact is certain that your former anarchical schemes and virulent conduct, had rendered you very exceptionable to some of the king's ministers. You have met with severe rebukes from them, and therefore were a very unfit person for this province to employ, even if another agent had been necessary.

Before I proceed to the next paragraph, I must beg leave to remind the reader, that you contend greatly for the justice of that form in our laws which requires "*the* "*truth*, the *whole truth*, and *nothing but the truth*, to be "spoken"; because, you say, "a falshood may destroy the "innocent, and so may *part of the truth* without the "whole." Will you now run contrary to a rule laid down by yourself? One would think not; but yet the next paragraph is one continued violation of it.

The Protestors had said, that, "the proposal of you as "an agent was extremely disagreeable to a very great "number of the most serious and reputable inhabitants "of this province, of all denominations and societies (ONE "proof of which is, your having been rejected both by "this city and county at the last election, &c.)"—Here the Protestors plainly mention this *rejection*, and that too in a parenthesis, only as ONE proof—But you honestly alter the sentence as follows *viz.*—"And THE Proof is my having been rejected, &c." making what they had suggested as only *one* proof to be the *whole* proof; whereas they had their own personal knowledge of your being disagreeable to the people, and petitions were then coming fast into the House to put the matter beyond all dispute, if there were any who doubted it.

Our Remarker goes on in the same manner transgressing his form laid down, and boasts, that in the county-election some who were chosen had scarce a score more votes than he; but does not say a word of the election for the city, where he was rejected by a great majority, though he had "represented it in Assembly for fourteen years," which was the very argument of the Protestors; so that if what he says of the county election were the *truth*, it is only *part of the truth*, and not the *whole truth*.

In like manner when he says, "do you, honourable sir, "reproach me with this, who for almost twice fourteen "years have been rejected (*if not being chosen is to be re-*"*jected*) by the same people, and unable with all your "wealth and connections to obtain an election in the "county where you reside, and the city where you were "born?" Would not one think from this, that the gentleman here meant, had for nearly twenty-eight years been set up at every election, and pushed as a candidate for the city and county of Philadelphia, with all the interest of his friends, as the Remarker was at the last election; and that old decrepit men had been carried out of their beds to vote for him; that his party had offered to the opposition to give up any, or all of the other nine Members to keep but this one man *in;* and that, after all, the gentleman had never once been chosen in the *county where he was born?* It would have required all this to make the case similar, and all this the Remarker no doubt would have to be understood. And yet the truth is, that the gentleman who he says has been thus rejected "*in the county where he was born*" was annually chosen to represent it for nine or ten years, by the almost unanimous voice of the people; that he then voluntarily resigned his seat, and never was a candidate for that county since, but once during the late war, when his friends proposed him, as a person whose presence in the House they then thought necesary for the king's service, and the defence of their much distressed country. Another remarkable difference is, that when the gentleman consented at last to come a second time into the House, he was chosen at once by two counties of their own free motion; whereas the Remarker has been rejected in two places at once, *viz.* both in this populous county and city, which pay half the taxes of the province. Nay farther; since the general election, when a resignation of some of his adherents was talked of, in order to give him a chance in two other counties, they were given to understand, that the principal inhabitants of these counties would oppose him to the utmost of their power; that they had good men within their own counties to represent them, and would not bear the reproach of taking in a man thrown out by the city and principal county of the province; and indeed so justly obnoxious is this man's name, that there is no place in Pennsylvania, where at this day he could have the least chance of any election.

But to proceed, the Protestors have said further, that his proposed appointment as an assistant agent "gave "them the more lively affliction as taken at the very "moment when they were informed by a member of the "House, that the governor had assured him, he had "received instructions from the proprietaries, on their "hearing of the late dispute (about the meaning of the "royal decree) to give his assent to the taxation of their "estates in the same manner as the estates of other per- "sons are to be taxed, and to confirm for the public use, "the several squares claimed by the city." Well! and if this was the ground of the dispute, was it not high time to drop it, and to rescue the province from the vast expence and uneasiness attending it? Our ambassador does not presume to say the contrary; but then his embassy would have been spoiled. He observes also that the Protestors used too delicate expressions on this subject. They should have made use of his choice language, and said, that "this step was taken at the moment, the *"precious moment,* when the proprietaries (by virtue of "some strong dose) were *disgorging five public squares,* "which they had near forty years unjustly and dishon"ourably seized and detained, (swallowed and eat up it "should be) from the city."

This language he would have liked better, but unhappily it could not be used on the occasion. The words inserted in the Protest were a report from the governor's mouth, and unless the Member who communicated the matter, had been possessed of the same dextrous turn for misrepresentation and falsehood for which the Remarker is so distinguished, he could not report what the governor said in any other manner than that in which it was committed to him. Hence appears the absurdity of charging the terms of that paragraph, whatever their nature may be, either to the *politeness* or *unpoliteness* of the *Protesters,* who only stated a matter of fact as they had received it.

The truth is, as I have been credibly informed, that in the first draught of the Protest, the words "given to the "city" stood instead of the words "claimed by the city." But in reading it over afterwards, the gentleman who brought the report, desired the expression might be altered and put in the terms he had it from the governor; who said that he had instructions relative to the confirmation of the squares "claimed by the city." For if they had been sufficiently granted before, nothing more would have been now necessary. The whole matter stands as follows. The founder of this province, fond of the regular and beautiful plan of his city, and looking forward to its future extent and improvement, may no doubt have intended (and mentioned his intention) to have five public squares in it, two on the Delaware side, two on the Schuylkill side, and one in the centre. His suffering his Surveyor General to publish a plan of the city, and all its proposed streets from river to river, leaving these squares open, is a sufficient presumption of this; and though they were never made a part of the original concessions to the people, nor formally granted to them, nor even publickly promised, by any evidence that appears, but seem only to be intended of his own free motion, both for ornament and use;—nevertheless from the circumstances above mentioned, it is not denied but the city might have a right to claim and expect them. But still this amounted only to a *claim*, and the present proprietors have not disputed it. Far from *seizing* and *detaining* them for forty years; the city has all that time had the use of them, and now has it. One of them has long ago been applied by the city itself to the public use, as a *Potter's field*, and *negroe burying ground*. The other *four* (*except some part of one of them) remain open for the city; and the Proprietors, in pursuance of what appears to have been their father's intention, have now given certain orders relative to the confirmation of them; which it seems must not be received as a matter of favor, nor even the ratification of a just *claim*, but a *disgorging* and *spewing* up. With what a

---

* Even this part is granted to a publick and pious use, as a burying ground to a German congregation in this city. The warrant and survey are of an old date; and it may be fairly presumed that if the part so granted had been deemed at the time to be within any of the proposed squares, this congregation would neither have petitioned for it, nor accepted of it, unless burying grounds were understood to be one of the publick uses for which these squares were originally designed.

wicked and virulent spirit is this remarker posses'd? What calumny and misrepresentation will he stick at, in order to inflame and divide? If here on the spot, he will shamefully assert what every person who will walk a few hundred yards may see with his own eyes to be *false*, what wicked calumny may it not be expected he will propogate of the good people of this province as well as the proprietors, to carry his points in England, where he may not expect an immediate detection?

Much in the like manner does he argue about the taxation of the proprietors. He has, for many years, poured forth volumes of abuse against them for *not consenting* to have their estates taxed as other people's were: and now he abuses them as much *for consenting* to it. The truth is, that the proprietors had proposed, among the first land-tax bills we had, that their estates should be taxed in the same manner as those of the people by persons named in the body of the bill, (as they had no voice in the choice of assessors and commissioners) which is strictly agreeable to the parliamentary mode of the land-tax, and was judged to be just and reasonable by the subsequent decree of the king in council. But when the Assembly would not even submit to this decree, but insisted on explaining one particular article in their own sense, the proprietors still willing to cultivate harmony, as soon as they heard of this new dispute, gave orders to admit the Assembly's own sense of the matter. Yet after all these concessions, and whether they do right or wrong, they are alike to incur the obloquy of this inflammatory and virulent man, whose views are not those of peace and reconciliation. It is therefore a good reason, which the Protestors offered, against employing him as an agent in our affairs *viz.* "That they believed his "fixed enmity to the proprietaries will preclude all "accommodation of our disputes with them, even on "equitable and reasonable terms." He does not deny this enmity, (tho' he asks the Protestors the reason of their belief;) for he proposes the terms on which his *enmity* is to cease. I never doubted but his mouth, foul as it is, might be stopped; but I believe, (and if he asks the reasons, I will tell them) that it cannot be done on quite so *disinterested* terms as he mentions. But, be that as it may, certainly there was room to think that a professed enemy to the proprietors, was very unlike to accommodate disputes, which he hath long and industriously worked up with unexampled calumny, unless we believe he designedly worked them up, to have the merit of appeasing them again: and if this be the case, we have been too long deluded by this crafty ambitious man.

I come then, as he does, in the next place, to what he calls the high charge of the Protestors, *viz.* "That he "heretofore ventured, *contrary* to an act of Assembly to "place the publick money in the Stocks, whereby this "province suffered a loss of £6000; and that sum added "to the £5000 granted for his expences, makes the whole "cost of his former voyage to England, amount to *eleven* "*thousand pounds.*"

This is a very high charge indeed, and if the Protestors had been fond of magnifying, they might with truth have added to the account, *commissions* paid him for receiving the money at the treasury, and sundry other articles, which would have swelled the account of his expenses to upward of *twelve thousand pounds.* This charge deserved something more like an answer than what he has been given.

It is a mean evasion to say, the *Bank* could not receive the money on the terms of the Act. And pray could it be placed in the *Stocks* on the terms of the act? He knows it could not. If then it had been kept in the Bank, the spirit and design of the act would have been complied with, though the terms had not been strictly fulfilled. But by placing it in the Stocks, the terms of the act were not only violated, but the spirit of it likewise, added to a vast loss occasioned thereby to the province.

The partizans of the Remarker may pretend they do not see this clearly. I will therefore endeavour to explain a little further. We all know that by the usage of the Bank, whoever deposits money there must subscribe their name, or write what is called their *Firm* at the Bank, for the greater security in drawing the money out; and we do not pretend that the trustees of the loan-office were to be transported to England to sign the books. No more did the trustees of the loan-office go to 'Change-Alley to receive a transfer of stock for the public money. All this was to be done by agents or reputable merchants living in London, who were to answer the draughts of the trustees, which they could have done as well by placing the money in the Bank as in the Stocks. When money is placed in the Bank no loss can happen: and if it possibly could, the persons who placed it there are not accountable for it; and therefore the Bank is the place where all persons entrusted with the custody of any public cash, chuse to deposit it; but if such persons, without authority, place it in the stocks, it is at their own risque, and as they may claim the profit of any rise of the Stocks, they are accountable for any loss that may happen by their falling.

Our Remarker tries to impose on the publick by saying "the House adopted the measure of placing the "money in the Stocks, and even passed a bill directing "the subsequent sums granted by Parliament to be placed "with the former." Now who would not think by this that he had been indemnified by law for placing the first money in the Stocks, and had by law placed the subsequent sums with it? Every person who reads what he has written, and entertains any opinion of his veracity, would believe this to be the case. And yet all he says is a wilful imposition. Had he chosen to tell the truth, and the *whole truth*, he would have added, that though the House did frame such a bill, it was never passed into a Law; that none of the subsequent sums granted by Parliament were ever placed in the Stocks, but in the hands of some reputable merchants in London, the legislature of this province not chusing to entrust him with those sums, after having abused his trust with regard to the money he had already received; which last sums were accordingly drawn out of the hands of these merchants, when the public service required, without the least loss to the province. He therefore remains alone accountable for the heavy loss on the first sums, which never would have happened if the law had been regarded; and no authority of any committee of the House, or even the whole Body, could dispense with a positive Law. And though I will not say, that he ought to *disgorge* a *loss*, as he makes the proprietors *disgorge five publick squares*, yet he ought to be made to refund this loss to the good people of this province, labouring under heavy debts on account of this and other parts of his conduct; it being of no consequence to them whether he brought this loss upon them by the spirit of gaming, or the spirit of pride, in figuring with the reputation of so much money placed by him in the publick funds.

If the exchange was higher at the time of drawing out

the money than at the time of purchasing the Stock, it was an accident; and it might have happened to be lower, and so the loss would have been encreased. There was a necessity of drawing it out in aid of the supplies of this province. The money was granted by parliament for this very purpose, to ease us of part of our heavy burthens, and not to go a jobbing with, for the uncertain prospect of profit, which might never arise. The *drawing* the money out, which he seems very angry at, was not so *imprudent* a step as he is pleased to call it. It was a very prudent and necessary one. The people of this province could not very patiently bear the burthen of new taxes, to humour him in an illegal measure, nor remain easy while so much of their money lay in the name of any private man, however great their opinion of his integrity might be, when in case of death, they could not have received the money, without the delay and expence of an act of parliament.

Having already shown that he has violated the form he laid down, in concealing part of the truth; I would next observe that he has again transgressed it, by saying more than the truth. In hopes to alleviate this charge against him, on account of the heavy loss to the province, he says to the chief justice,—"you, honourable Sir, "(my enemy of seven years standing) were appointed on "the committee for examining my ACCOUNTS; you reported "that that you found THEM *just*, and signed the report."

Now what can any one understand from this, but that the Chief Justice signed a report, approving all the accounts of this man's Agency, even including the money placed in the Stocks, &c., &c. And yet in the report there is no such word as ACCOUNTS in the plural number, or ACCOUNT in general. It mentions only *one account* of particular expence compared with vouchers amounting to £714, 10s, 7d ; which was the only *account* submitted to the committee: "In obedience to the order of the "House we have examined the ACCOUNT of Benjamin "Franklin, Esq ; with the vouchers to us produced, and "find that he has expended &c."—These are the words of the report; and it requires a very uncommon force of logic to construe the signing of this report upon a particular account into a justification of all his conduct in his agency.

With the like truth a little afterwards, speaking of the gentleman above referred to, he says—"you, Sir, of all "others was the very Member that proposed, for the "honor and justice of the House, a compensation to be "made of the *five thousand pounds* you mention." If this were true, he has made the gentleman a very ungrateful return for this, as well as many former favours. But it happens to be a gross falshood. The gentleman has publickly declared, that when the matter was first mentioned, it was only by some of the Members in occasional conversation at the committee, before whom it could not come as a matter of business; that those Members spoke of the reasonableness of making the *Remarker* some compensation for what they called his services in England, and mentioned an agent that had been allowed at the rate of *five hundred pounds sterling per annum*, by the colony of Virginia; which agent resided in England and could attend to his other business, whereas Mr. Franklin was forced to leave his family, and quit valuable business here. To which the said gentleman, *viz.* the chief justice replied, that he thought it a very great allowance, but at length acquiesced with what appeared to be the sentiments of a great majority of the committee, the matter not being then before them, as hath been observed. And when this business came into the House, it is notoriously known, that the motion was made, not by the chief justice, but by several of the *Remarker's* friends, and by a member of Chester county in particular, who further proposed that every expence of the Remarker during his whole absence, should be defrayed by the House. This was strenuously opposed by the chief justice, who said he had no fellowship with him nor his politicks, that he never had approved of sending the Member to England, nor saw any benefit the Province had received by it, that he had spent a great deal of time and money in parading about to different parts of England, and even into Scotland, and must necessarily be at a large expence in maintaining his son, which were matters this province had nothing to do with. But that notwithstanding, since the House had thought fit to employ him on an idle errand, he thought they were now obliged in *honour and justice* to make him a reasonable allowance; and *five hundred pounds sterling, per annum*, being the least sum mentioned by any body, he said that he would not object to it, tho' he thought the allowance rather too large.

This is a candid and circumstantial account of this matter, in which the Member acted as became an honest man; and the reader may judge how base a part the Remarker acts, in the false invidious turn he gives to the affair.

Equally malicious and groundless is the accusation he brings against the gentleman for "concealing instructions "which he was said to bring from the proprietors"—for healing our differences; of which accusation a great handle has been made for party views.

Whoever will suffer himself to reflect for a moment, will see the absurdity of thinking that ever instructions of this kind could be given to be communicated to the province, by a private gentleman, while the proprietors had a governor (one of their own family) on the spot. These instructions were not a moment *concealed*, nor was it necessary to communicate them in any other manner than they were.

If the words of the royal decree (which were inserted verbatim in the latter act) were so clear, as the Assembly contest, that they could not be understood in any other sense but that which they contended for, there was nothing to hinder the act from being executed in that sense, if the proprietors had never given any instructions at all on that head. But to put the matter out of doubt, and to remove all cause of uneasiness, they were pleased to give instructions to the governor to acquaint the proper officers, that the law might be executed accordingly. This was all that was wanted; no new law was necessary. Nothing remain'd but to let the Assembly know that such instructions were given, and this was done by a Member, from the governors own mouth. Had the Assembly been willing or desirous to receive any further information, they might have obtained it by sending a very short message; for messages have often passed on matters of as little importance.

The chief justice, it is true, was in London when the instructions were sent. He was there made acquainted with them, and approved of them as just and tending to peace. It is not improbable but on his coming over he might be charged by the proprietors with letters to the governor on the subject, but he is known to have solemnly declared that he never was invested with any powers or commissions from the proprietors, to communicate their intentions to the House, or to settle any difference between them. But every Member, nay every private man who conversed with him, can testify, that he did not keep the proprietors' intentions secret. What is asserted in the extract of Mr. Barclay's letter, quoted by the Remarker, must therefore have been founded on some mistake.

Thus have I followed the *Remarker* through every thing that bears the least appearance of argument in his performance; and if the *Protesters* meet with no more formidable attack than this, their arguments will remain fully convincing to cool and deliberate minds. And though he exults in carrying with him the sanction of *two* to *one* in the House, which is a misrepresentation also; yet let him take into the account, that he carries with him the bitter reproaches and indignation of at least *five* to *one* of an injured people.

Before I leave the *Protest*, let me observe that there is one part of it, which it did not suit him to mention.

The Protesters (after using their utmost endeavours against burthening this province with any more agents than one, and particularly against employing this man, who seems too ready to traffick our singular privileges away for gratifying his own ambition and resentment) frankly proposed in condescension to their Brethren, who *thought* another *agent necessary*, to concur with them in the appointment of any person of weight and integrity in London; and in order to save the expence to the province, already burden'd with heavy taxes, they further proposed that it should be by subscription, to which they generously offered to contribute their quotas, if the other members would do the same.

I now proceed to a more disagreeable part of my Task; *viz*, to take some notice of the gross slander and scurrility of this Remarker.

And first then, because he himself (the most unpopular and odious name in the province) lost his election, wherever it was attempted to set him, he therefore abuses almost the whole body of the people.

"The *superiority*," he says, "was obtained over him at "the expence of honour and conscience, by exasperating "the ignorant, by falsehoods, by prejudices, &c." One set of men who opposed him meaning his majesty's faithful subjects the *Presbyterians*, (who have ever been among the foremost in defending their country, and promoting their sovereign's measures; while this virulent calumniator, and many of his present adherents, thought they did us a great favor in permitting us to spill our own blood, and spend our own money, in the publick cause) this numerous and loyal people are called "*relig-* "*ious* bigots, *of all savages the most bruitish.*"

The industrious GERMANS, to whom this province is so much indebted for its flourishing state, and who have suffered so much from this man's ill-timed disputes, that they thought him unworthy of further trust—they too are called by him "*a wretched rabble, brought to swear* "*themselves intituled to a vote.*" Much in the same manner he had treated them on a former occasion ; calling them "a set of *boors herding together,*" as if he was speaking of *swine.* Yet this valuable body of men are true subjects to his majesty ; have cultivated a great extent of our country under the faith of our *charter*, are possessed of large property, and entitled to the privileges of Englishmen and a vote by our laws ; and have exercised these their rights, without interruption, for many years.

The members of the church of England have at present escaped his calumny. He considered, perhaps, the country to which he was going, and may hope to carry some future points by his complaisance. But he will probably be mistaken. For as he belongs to no religious society, and regards none, so he is alike detested by all, except one, and by many serious good men among that society also.

These are some specimens of his shameful and scandalous manner of treating the People of this province in general. To bestow any answer on such scurrility, would be ridiculous. None but a very bad man, or one delirious with rage, disappointment and malice, would utter such language, even against a single antagonist, much less against whole bodies of people; unsupported, as it is, with any shadow of reason. In the same manner, he treats the respectable names, who, in execution of what they judged their duty in their place, opposed his appointment. They are called—"proprietary "minions, making use of a new form of libelling, as the "vehicle of personal malice, &c." Yet the ten gentlemen who signed the Protest are known to be persons of the fairest character and men of fortune, absolutely independent of the proprietary family, holding no places under them, soliciting none, nor ever likely to accept of any. Out of this number, I should have excepted the Chief Justice, who has the trifling salary of about £120 sterling per annum, and that not depending on the proprietors, but on the yearly vote of the Assembly alone; which salary too, it is well known, he has constantly applied to publick or charitable uses. This office he accepted only thro' the earnest entreaties and persuasions of many good men, and after repeated refusals to serve in it. He has since often desired leave of the several governors to resign it, on account of his advanced age and bodily infirmities, and still wishes to do it as soon as his superiors can be prevailed on to fill it up with another.

As the chief force of the Remarker's virulence seems directed against this gentleman. I shall take the liberty to state the account between them, a little more particularly.

The gentleman, I presume, does not pretend an exemption from human failings. His open and candid temper may have led him more than once, to rely too easily on the professions of false and insidious men; and he is, in no instance, more chargeable with this, than in what he has done for this ungrateful incendiary, who, probably, had never been of consideration enough to give the least disturbance to this province, but for the numerous favours so ill bestowed on him, by this gentleman and his friends. They were the persons who first raised him from his original obscurity, and got him appointed *Printer* to the province, and *Clerk* to the house of assembly. Not resting here, the gentleman whom he has so grossly vilified, did likewise procure him the office of *joint-postmaster* of America, by means of his name-sake, the worthy RALPH ALLEN, Esq; of *Bath*, to whom this Remarker was utterly unknown.

He seemed for a time to carry some appearance of gratitude for these favors; and this gentleman and his friends continued their regard to him, till, at length, upon some slight which he supposed the proprietors had put upon him, in not answering one of his letters, and on some personal difference with GOVERNOR MORRIS, they found him all at once renouncing every principle he had formerly professed; openly attacking government, fomenting division, and joining himself avowedly to those, whom before he had often spoke of with the greatest contempt and disapprobation.

Then, indeed, the gentlemen dropped him; but they did it with a silent disregard; and he has not been without his moments of repentance for his conduct. He has made frequent overtures towards a reconciliation;

and, within these two years, has passed the most lavish encomiums on the gentleman who is the present object of his resentment; declaring that "*he even revered the ashes* "*of their former friendship.*"

But how strangely he must have forgot himself, when he says in his Remarks, that "the *dear delight* and con- "*stant employment* of the gentleman's life (the ashes of "whose former *friendship* he reveres) has been the maim- "ing or murdering all the reputations that stand in his "way?" A poor compliment this, which the Remarker pays to his own choice of friends! Is it possible that *he* could have had so many years close friendship with a person, the *dear delight* and *constant employment* of whose whole life has been of so infernal a nature? Into what monstrous absurdities and contradictions will the frantic rage of virulent men transport them?

To take further notice of this infamous slander, would be perfectly needless. It stands self-refuted; and there is not a character perhaps, in this province, to which it could less justly be applied. With regard to the chief justice of this province, his virtues are well known, and his character extended so greatly to his advantage through all parts of America, that it cannot receive the least injury from this vain and wicked attempt. The world is apt enough to fix blemishes and stains where there ought not to be any; nor will it suffer even a man's foibles to pass into oblivion; and surely, if the gentleman had been obnoxious to this heavy charge (and that through his whole life too) we could not but have heard of it before now. But the truth is, that "it was "not invented before," as the Remarker says on another occasion; and therefore the gentleman's character, re- mained untouched, till, in the rage of disappointment, this furious attack was made upon it, by venturing to spread the most glaring falshoods; falshoods which have made the Remarker's friends blush for him, and his enemies triumph. He, no doubt, felt the weight of this gentleman's reputation against him, and therefore thought it necessary to attempt a breach in it; but the blow has recoiled upon himself, and has wounded the credit of every other part of his performance. Thus, like the hunted beast, while he bites the spear of his pursuer, he breaks his own fangs.

With the like slander he insinuates, that endeavours have been used in this province, "to render his majesty's "government odious; that traiterous papers, to this "purpose, had been written and translated into other "languages; and that it had been declared, written and "printed, that the king's little finger we should find "heavier than the proprietors' whole loins, *with regard to* "*our liberties;*" and, by the whole reading of the paragraph, he seems to charge these "exploits" chiefly, if not solely, to the gentleman above-mentioned, as another mark of the "reverence he pays to the ashes of their "former friendship."

But it is happy for the gentleman reflected upon, that wherever his character is known, this charge will meet with as little regard as the former. Thro' his whole life, he has been a constant friend to government and order; an enemy to every factions and anarchical scheme, and a strenuous promoter of the king's service. Every one of his majesty's officers, from the commanders in chief, to the lowest subaltern, will be ready to acknowledge the particular encouragement and assistance they have on all occasions received from him, in every part of their duty; while the public service has been almost constantly obstructed by the licentious spirit of this turbulent Remarker.

The two Characters afford a most striking contrast. The Chief Justice, while in America, does his utmost to support government, and promote the king's service; and, when in England, he was equally zealous to support the Rights of America; with a firm and independent spirit, maintaining in behalf of the people here, that they considered it to be their essential right as British subjects, *to assess their own taxes;* and that any *law* to subject them to *internal taxations*, otherwise than by their own representatives, would be *disfranchising* them of the rights of englishmen: in which opinion, he has the concurring sentiments of, I believe, every representative body on this continent.

But very different is the conduct of our ambitious and time-serving remarker. Here in America, his delight is in contention, anarchy and opposition to government. And then, when he has created an embassy for himself, and gets on the other side of the Atlantic, he shifts with the scene; puts off the noisy demagogue, forgets the cause of his employers, truckles for preferment for himself and family, and boasts services he never performed.

As to any papers published at the late election, that could give the least colour to the charge he has brought, he or his adherents are called upon to shew them, and expressly to mention the passages, else to take the shame to themselves. I, for my part, have neither seen, or before heard of, any such; and as to the chief justice, who neither gave any vote, nor even stirr'd out of his house during the whole election, he has declared, that far from writing or publishing, he has not even read any thing written or published by either side, since his return from England, except the *Supplement to the Pennsylvania Journal*, which he never saw, till a printed copy was put into his hands by a friend, desiring him to peruse it, as he was mentioned in it. There is but one paragraph in that paper that makes any comparison between the privileges enjoyed here, and those in royal governments; and that paragraph, far from making such governments odious, has these express words, *viz.* "That no government under his sacred Majesty can be "an unhappy one; but that there are degrees of happi- "ness as well as privileges." This surely does not convey the least reflection against such governments.

The great founder of this province had the noble res- olution, many years ago, to tell his superiors, in behalf of his people, that "they had not followed him so far, to "lose a single tittle of the charter granted to them, or "of the great charter to which all Englishmen were "born." This he did without giving offence: and, I doubt not, if ever this Remarker should venture to push his daring attempts farther against the liberties of *Pennsylvania*, there will be those found who will be ready to plead with unshaken firmness, and without giving the least offence to the wise, equitable and august judicature before whom only this matter can come— "That when English colonies were first planted, and "men were to quit their native country, and, for the "extension of its commerce, to enter into what was then "considered as a kind of voluntary banishment; it was "thought proper to indulge and encourage them with "particular grants and privileges, suitable to their "circumstances.

"The first settlers of *Pennsylvania*, were highly "favoured in this respect by their humane founder, who "(under the ample authority of a royal charter) granted "them many singular privileges and immunities; to

"which the rapid growth of this province is to be prin-
"cipally ascribed. By the very name of these privileges,
"multitudes of people have been drawn from almost all
"quarters of the world ; who have encreased the number
"of British subjects, cultivated a wilderness, and made
"it one of the fairest and most valuable parts of his
"Majesty's American dominions. Having thus amply
"fulfilled the considerations for which these privileges
"were granted, they now think themselves entituled to
"the perpetual enjoyment of them. They have not
"forfeited them by any act of disloyalty to their most
"gracious sovereign ; nor are they pretended to be incon-
"sistent with the nature of government, or such as could
"not have been legally conveyed to them. They do now,
"therefore, claim these previleges *entire;* and a majority
"of at least *five* to *one* of them have publickly avowed
"that claim, and say that their charter, which is their
"birth right, has expressly put it out of the power of
"their Representatives, by themselves, to do any matter,
"or thing, whereby their privileges may be affected.
"Under such circumstances as these, when they see a
"change (unsought for by our indulgent Sovereign,
"unwished for by the people, and even notoriously
"repugnant to their general sentiments) I say, when
"under such circumstances, they see a measure of such
"immense importance, hurried wickedly and vehemently
"on, by the ambition of a single man, it is impossible
"but indignation and resentment must rise to their
"utmost heighth."

All this, I say, may be asserted without the least
offence. There is not a private corporation that would
not steadfastly say as much as this, in behalf of their most
inconsiderable immunities. And yet this is the amount
of all that is to be found in the papers which, for the

credit of his country, the Remarker has been pleased to call treasonable.

There is no such expression to be found in them, as that "the king's little finger we shall find *heavier* than "the proprietors' whole loins, *in regard to our liberties.*" The Remarker, with his usual candor, has added words of his own to the sentence; for what is there said, is not spoken, *with regard to our liberties*, but with regard to instructions. The Remarker has made it a charge, against *proprietary instructions,* that our judges were thereby prevented from having their commissions *during good behavior.* It is answered, that "we should find the "king's little finger thicker than the proprietor's whole "loins," with regard to the authority of instructions of this kind; and an instance is given of Mr. Hardy's case, who lost the government of *New Jersey* for appointing one judge during good behaviour.

It is true, many papers have been publish'd in this province, which, by comparison, have a tendency to "render royal governments odious," as well with respect to the tenor of Judges' commissions, as the tenor of militia-laws, the right of disposing the public money, and the appointment of the officers of the revenue, &c. —But it is the Remarker's misfortune, that these publications have had him for their author, and are striking specimens of his boasted loyalty, and "constant en-"deavours to promote the measures of the crown, ever "since he had any influence in the province." Nothing but his own matchless assurance could make him hope that this assertion could obtain any more credit in *England*, than it can in *America;* when it is incontestably known, that, for many years past, he has taken every advantage of the distresses of his country, to retard the public supplies, to wrest the prerogatives of the crown out of the hands of the King's representative, to strip the executive part of government of its constitutional authority, and to affect even royalty himself.

I shall not, in imitation of his example, advance such charges, without proof.

During the last war, he drew up with his own hand, and afterwards defended in his news-paper, a militia bill (which the governor in the distress of the country, was obliged to pass into a law) by which the nomination of the officers, and consequently the command of the militia, were wrested out of the hands of the king's representative; by which, the Remarker himself got elected to the office of colonel, paraded his regiment about the streets to intimidate his opponents; and on setting out and returning from journeys, was escorted with drawn swords, and received with rested arms, and other affectations of royal state; while the king's representative had nothing left, but to walk about, and look silently on.

This law being repealed by his majesty, our Remarker, in the profusion of his loyalty, had the assurance last spring, to get another presented to the governor, worse in many respects, than the former; still depriving the king's representative of the nomination of the officers, and even giving the provincial commissioners a *negative* on the direction of the operations of the militia. The governor having refused to pass this bill, he was charged (in a paper published under the Remarker's patronage at the last election) with being a tyrant, and being led by wicked proprietary* instructions, to subject the people to grievous fines and *death* by military courts; to refuse them the choice of their own officers, and the benefit of being tried for military offences in the civil

---

*See a paper call'd Reasons why the late Militia Bill miscarried. See also the resolves of March the 24th last.

courts, by a jury nominated by a sheriff of their own election; notwithstanding the governor, by his amendments, only desired the bill to be rendered conformable to the militia laws in all the governments around us, declaring that he would not pass it otherwise, as contrary to a known and positive determination of the king in council.

Surely "these exploits of our Remarker, are not for a "man that holds a profitable office under the crown; "and as he says, can expect to hold it no longer than he "behaves with the fidelity and duty that becomes every "good subject.§" But yet these are not half of his loyal "exploits."

His majesty has repealed a law (pas'd by our infamous Governor *Denny*) appointing our judges *during good behaviour*. The Remarker was then our agent and plenipotentiary at London, and either could not, or did not think it safe for him there to oppose that repeal; yet still this "faithful and dutiful subject," (as he calls himself) *resolves* it to be among the list of our grievances, and *unjust*, that the proprietors, in obedience to the king's determination, should "appoint judges during "*their* pleasure." Again, though it be expressly subversive of the royal prerogative and unconstitutional, for an assembly to claim the appointment of officers in the *civil* and *executive* part of the government, or the sole disposition of the public money, accountable, as they are, only to themselves; nay tho' his majesty has repealed a law, on this very account; yet this man has constantly taken advantage of his country's distress, violently to repeat all these claims. By these means he has often endeavoured to deny the Governor even a voice in the disposition of the public money: and has got the nom-

---
§See remarks, page 89.

ination of the officers of the revenue, and even military officers, such as barrick-masters, &c. taken out of the hands of the King's representative.

These are some of the dutiful *exploits* which our Remarker has performed; and tho' he thought it his Interest to boast great loyalty, when he was setting out for England: yet his superiors there, to whom these things are well known, will be at no loss to form a right judgment concerning him. I could now proceed to give some striking Instances of his loyalty, extracted from his writing as a private man; in which he has treated his Majesty's *publick Boards, and royal Instructions*, much in the same bitter and licentious manner, as he treats the powers of government here.—"It is not, says he, ‡ to be presumed that *such* as have been long accustomed to "consider the colonies in general, as only so many "dependencies on the *Council-Board*, the *Board of Trade* "and the *Board of Customs;* or as a hot-bed for causes, "jobbs and other pecuniary emoluments, and bound as "effectually by *instructions* as by *laws*, can be prevailed "on to consider these *patriot-rusties* (of Pennsylvania) "with any degree of respect."

But having already exceeded the length I intended, I shall not take further notice of this man as a writer. It is however to be hoped that some person of more leisure may, for the sake of an abused Province, give a compleat account of his conduct ever since it was the misfortune of this country that he had any influence in it. There is ample room to shew how diametrically opposite his principles have been at different times; how he has paid servile court to all sides, deceived all, calumniated all! How he has been endeavouring, first with one party, then with another, to pave the way to his present attempt!

‡Historical review of Pennsylvania.

what misrepresentations he has spread, and what ferments he has worked up for this purpose!

It might likewise be shewn, by what means, after his schemes had rendered him odious to every other society in the province, he has formed a party in *one*, by sowing divisions among them; and tho' they have heretofore been thought remarkable for their sagacity and prudence, yet he has craftily drawn their young men into his measures; lessening the influence of the serious and considerate part of their body; and, under the mark of friendship, hurrying them on to that ruin, which he had before endeavoured to bring upon them, in open enmity.

This would furnish a character, not such as is given in the *lapidary* way, to which he has of late been accustomed; but such as will be preserved in the more lasting strokes of faithful history.

At present I shall conclude only with a *sketch;* and that he may not call it either "maiming or murdering" —I shall give part of it in his own *drawing;* and part of it in the drawing of a celebrated english poet. The reader may make the application where he pleases; for I cannot tell for whom the latter part was designed.

"Tho* foiled and disgraced, this *Anti-Penn*, this under-
"taker to subvert the building *Penn* had raised, is far
"from quiting the lists. On the contrary, he lies in wait
"with impatience for the verification of his own pre-
"dictions———Factions he has found means to form,
"both in the city and in several counties. Tools and
"implements of all kinds he has———The prostitute
"writer, the whispering incendiary, the avowed des-
"perado, surround him. The press he has made an
"outrageous use of; a cry he has raised; and, in minia-

---

*See the Remarker's historical review, page 274-5.

"ture, the whole game of faction has been here played
"by him, &c."
   "*Paleness,* † not such as on his wings
   "The messenger of sickness brings,
   "But such as takes its coward rise,
   "From conscious baseness, conscious vice,
   "O'erspread his cheeks;—*disdain* and *pride,*
   "To upstart fortunes ever tied,
   "Scowl'd on his brow;—within his eye,
   "Insidious, lurking like a spy
   "To caution principled by fear,
   "Not daring open to appear,
   "Lodged covert *mischief; passion* hung
   "On his lips quivering; on his tongue
   "*Fraud* dwelt at large; within his breast
   "All that makes villain found a nest.

---

†CHURCHILL.

INDEX.

Abercombie, General . 35
Alarm after Braddock's defeat . 28, 30, 31, 33
Alexander, James . 61
Alexander, James Mrs. 42
Allen, Andrew . 3, 45, 49, 50, 55, 56
Allen, Anne . 3, 48, 68
Allen, James . 3, 45, 49, 50, 55, 56
Allen, John . 3, 38, 39, 42, 44, 46, 47, 48, 51, 53
Allen, Margaret 58, 76, 79
Allen, Ralph . . 120
Allen, William . 3, 40, 48, 50, 52, 55, 57, 59, 74, 79, 85, 93, 97, 102, 113, 116, 119, 120, 122, 123 Salary of . 119
Allen, William Mrs. . 3, 37, 43
Ambler, Mrs. . . 48

Arms ordered . . 23
Arthur, Joseph . . 14
Ashton, Ralph . . 35
Assembly . 36, 37, 57, 64, 73, 74, 82, 109, 116
Bacon, Anthony . 68
Baldwin, Mr. . . . 78
Bank, proposed . . 58
Barclay, Alexander . 56
Barclay, David 15, 41, 44, 47, 61, 62, 76, 117
Barclay, John . . 58
Barre, Colonel . . 64
Baynton, Mr. . . . 9
Bellair's Lands . 6, 14, 17
Bernard, Governor . 74
Bolitho 55
Books and Pamphlets 12, 24, 36, 71, 78
Borrowing Money . 16
Braddock's Defeat . 22
Bricks imported . . 20
Bryan, George . . 85

Budd, John . . . 54
Budd, Mary . . . 3
Budd, Susanna . . 3
Budd, Thomas . . 3
Burd, Edward . . 4
Burd, Sarah . . . 4
Butler and Matthews 10

Cambric, imported . 36
Campbell, Mr. Hume 24
Carey, I. & P. . . . 11
Carpets, imported . 68
Change from Proprietary to Royal Government proposed 64, 82, 124, 125
Child, Charles . . 36
Churchill quoted . 131
Coach . . . 11, 13, 16
Cockshals, Mr. . . 69
Coleman, William . 9, 75
Copper Mine . 18, 19, 20, 21, 29
Curtains imported . 68

De-Lancey, James . 3
Denny, Governor . . 128
Dickinson, John . . 85
Dickinson, Jonathan 45
Drummond, Mr. . . 74
Dun, Capt. 34

Election . 56, 63, 83, 90, 104, 106, 118, 123
Ellebank, Lord . . 60
England, Disputes with . 70, 72, 73, 74
England, Oppressions by . 65, 66, 67, 75, 77
English Stock . 43, 47, 48, 52, 66

Exports 17
Ferguson, Robert . 10
Fielding, Sir John . 58
Fisher, Governor . . 20
Forbes, General . 38, 40
Forester, Mr. . . . 24
Fothergill, Dr. . . 60, 85
Fox, Joseph . . . 97
Franklin, Benjamin . 4, 10, 49, 57, 62, 63, 81, 82, 83, 84, 87, 88, 91, 97, 98, 99, 103, 114, 117, 123, 130
Franks, David . . 42
French, Aggressions of 7, 17, 28
French Vessels captured 29

Gage, Lord . . 53, 66
Galloway 57
Germans . 25, 27, 118
Gibson, John . 15, 34, 40
Gordon, William . 31
Gun, new 67

Hacket 44, 69
Hamilton, Andrew . 3
Hamilton, Governor James . . 34, 37, 38, 49, 51, 62, 64, 65, 67, 71
Hamilton, Margaret . 3
Handbury, Capel . 69, 70
Hardy, Mr. . . . 126
Henry, William . . 18
Hick, Mr. 69
Hubley, Misses . . 4
Hughes, John . . 97
Hunt, John . . 56, 63
Hunter . . . 10, 11
Hyde, Lord . . . 62

Importations . 12, 20,
24, 36, 41, 42, 48, 58, 59,
61, 68, 71, 78, 79
Indians, Murders by
24, 28, 33, 91
Indians, Purchase
from . . 6, 7, 14, 17
Instructions 115, 126, 127
Irish, Anna . . . 35
Irish, Nathaniel . . 35
Ironworks . 43, 44, 69
Jackson, Mr. . 57, 62, 85
Jackson & Rutherford 51
James, Abel . . . 63
Jersey Lands 7, 8, 9, 53
Jesuits Bark . . . 20
Judges Commissioned
during pleasure . 128
Keppele, Henry . . 85
King, Petition to the
24, 26, 32
Lamar, Mrs. . . . 58
Lands . . 6, 7, 8, 9, 14,
15, 17, 53
Lawn, imported . . 36
Lea, Mr. 70
Letters to
Arrecharreta, Don
Juan 17
Barclay, D . 5, 9, 12,
15, 18, 20, 22, 24, 28,
33, 34, 35, 36, 37, 38,
42, 43, 44, 45, 47, 48,
49, 50, 51, 52, 55, 56,
62, 65, 66, 67, 70, 71,
74, 76, 79
Barclay, John . 18, 29
Beckford, William 31
Butler, Edmund . 14
Carey, I. & P. . . 9

Chiswell, Col. John 16
Davis, Robert 61, 71, 78
Drummond, Colin 74
Farmer & Galton . 67
Griffiths, John 43, 44
Hopkins, William 52
Hume, B. . . . 5
Jackson & Rutherford . . . 39, 42
Nelson, Wm. . 35, 48
Paris, Ferdinand 24, 30
Patterson, Evan . 6,
14, 17
Pitt, William . . 58
Ruiz, Don Bernardo 11,
13, 15, 16, 17, 20, 29
Simpson, Thos. . 7, 53
Tysson, Francis . 45
Wade, John . . 34
Walker, Samuel . 69
Lisbon, Letter to . 17
Logan, James . . 45
Lottery Tickets 5, 10, 15
Loudon, Lord . . . 35
McCall, Samuel . . 14
McCanaughy, D. . 85
Maddox, Mr. . . . 9
Magnolia Roots . . 66
Mann, Sir Horace . 40
Medicine 17
Militia Law . . 30, 32,
33, 127
Mine . 18, 19, 20, 21, 29
Money borrowed on interest 16
Money, public invested
vested in stock . 84,
95, 110, 111
Monkton, John . . 36
Montgomery, John . 85

Moore, John . . . 97
Morris, Governor . 120
Morton, John . . 97
Mytton, John . . . 53
Nelson, Mr. . . . 48
Norris, Mr. . . . 96
Ore 20, 21
Oswald, Miss . . . 76
Paper Money . . . 37
Paris, Ferdinand . . 35
Pearson, Isaac . . 97
Penn family . . 25, 54,
  57, 60, 62, 64, 66, 82,
  92, 109, 116
Pewter Plates . . . 20
Philadelphia, Squares
  in . 83, 92, 107, 108
Pine Buds for Gout 58,
  59, 61, 66
Pitt, William . 58, 59, 62
Plumley, Sarah . . 3
Plumsted, William . 42
Possant, Captain . . 14
Postmastership, Franklin's appointment
  10, 120
Powell, Captain . . 70
Pratt, Chief Justice . 62
Presents . . . 11, 15
Protest . . 81, 88, 102
Quakers . 25, 27, 32, 33

Redman, Dr. . . . 35
Remarks by Franklin 87
Rhoads, Samuel . . 97
Ring, Mourning . . 43
Roaque, Mr. . . . 61
Robertson 66
Robinson, Captain . 30
Ross, Dr. 20
Ross, John 97

Rum 9
Rutherford, Captain 42
Saunders, Isaac . . 85
Scotch-Irish People . 25
Scott, Col. 77
Seeds . . . 52, 53
Shelborn, Lord . . 65
Shippen, Edward . 3, 4
Shippen, Joseph 38, 39, 68
Shirley 14
Silver, Value of Falls 52
Simpson . . . 5, 8, 54
Slave, a fugitive . . 58
Sloop Watts captured 14
Smith, William . . 4
Southwell, Edward . 53
Stamp Act 67
Stanwix, General . 40
Strettell, Amos . . 85
Stuart, Alexander . 11, 50
Sydenham, Mr. . . 20
Tabb, Mr. 48
Taylor, George . . 85
Thinn, Captain . . 18
Trade, in America,
  poor 65
Turner, Mr. . . 43, 77
Vegetables . 12, 22, 34
Wages 30, 70
Walker, L. L. . . . 4
Waters, Mr. . . . 48
West, Benjamin . 3, 41,
  42, 47, 51
Wigs 5, 36
Wilkinson, John . . 97
Willing, Thos. . . 85
Wine 48
Wynn, Thomas . . 53
Yellow Fever . . . 52
York, Mr. 24

www.ingramcontent.com/pod-product-compliance
Lightning Source LLC
Chambersburg PA
CBHW022133160426
43197CB00009B/1259